KU-191-452

William Ogilvie's

BIRTHRIGHT

in

LAND

*Honour
thy father and
thy mother that thy
days may be long upon
the* LAND
which the Lord thy God
giveth thee.
-BIRTHRIGHT
TENURE!

LONDON

Othila Press

1997

Birthright in Land published in this form by Othila Press, 58a Abingdon Road, London, W8 6AP, England.

© Land Reform Scotland 1997

The texts, particularly the *Forenotes*, some of the editors' notes, and the use of some quotations, draw on the work of previous unpublished Scottish Ogilvie Society editions of *Birthright in Land*. *Foreword: Scotland and the Land Question* © Roger Sandilands 1996. *Introduction: Our Birthright in Land* © Peter Gibb 1997. *MacDonald's Preface*, by DC MacDonald, first published by Kegan Paul, Trench, Trübner & Co. Ltd., London, in 1891, as part of *Birthright in Land:* this edition by George Morton 1997. *An Essay on the Right of Property in Land, &c.*, by William Ogilvie, first printed for J Walter, Charing Cross, London, in 1782, and issued anonymously: this edition by Peter Gibb 1997. *MacDonald's Biographical Notes*, by DC MacDonald, first published as *Biographical Notes, with Side Issues, by the Editor*, by Kegan Paul, Trench, Trübner & Co., Ltd., London, in 1891, as part of *Birthright in Land:* this edition by George Morton 1997. *The Rev. Maister Whatefer's Chronicle of Strathconon*, by DC MacDonald, first published by Kegan Paul, Trench, Trübner & Co. Ltd., London, in 1891, as part of *Birthright in Land* (within the *Biographical Notes*): this edition by Peter Gibb 1997. *Afterword: The Global Green Tax? Community Ground Rent* © Peter Gibb 1997.

All Rights Reserved

BRITISH LIBRARY CATALOGUING IN PUBLICATION
Ogilvie, William (1736-1819)
Birthright in Land

    1. Popular Scottish Politics
    2. Land Reform   3. Political Economy
    I. Title   II. Ogilvie, William, *Birthright in Land,* with Biographical Notes by DC MacDonald, 1891
     III. Anonymous, *An Essay on the Right of Property in Land*, 1782

    ISBN 1 901647 13 7

Book design, layout and production by Peter Gibb. Cover photomontage by Peter van den Berg.

Printed and bound in Great Britain by MFP Design & Print, Manchester.
Paper is *New World*, 90 gsm., 100% recycled from printed waste and not rebleached, manufactured by the Silverton Mill, Hele, Devon, England.

Othila Press
acknowledges with gratitude
Shirley - Anne Hardy's   inspiration
in   retrieving   from   undeserved   obscurity
the   seminal   essay   by   William   Ogilvie,
and   also   her   work   on   DCMacDonald's
Biographical   Notes   and   associated   texts.
The   economic   principles   articulated
in the essay need to be re-evaluated
so   that   policies   for   reshaping
Scotland's destiny are developed
on the basis of
enlightened   wisdom.

The   publisher   is   also   grateful   to

Sally Blewett, Graeme Curran, John Digney, Peter Gibb, Paul Gill,
Karen Grant, Fred Harrison, Ian Lambert, George Morton, Charlie Riddell,
JJ Robertson, Roger Sandilands, David Shields, Jane Shields, Ian Sillars,
John Stocks, Morag Stocks, Roger Ward, Suzl Ward,
Anthony Werner and Helen Young

for their assistance with this project.

This publication has been made possible by grants from the
Scottish Ogilvie Society and the Scottish League for Land Value Taxation.

To
four lovers of mankind

Robert Burns

Henry George

DC MacDonald

William Ogilvie

Contents

" The earth has sworn unto the day of Paradise that all truths will come to the light sooner or later. "

A Sufi saying

In the summer of 1994, a small group of people, then largely strangers to each other, were brought together in a small cottage high up in highland Perthshire. Their shared political interest was in the land and tax-reform ideas of the turn-of-the-century American political-economist *Henry George*; and the gathering had been called to share in the rediscovery of the *suppressed* masterwork of Aberdeen's own 'proto-Georgist', the "rebel professor" - *William Ogilvie*. The crucial political relevance of William Ogilvie *to Scotland today* became clear, and the Gathering resolved to republish his work. It is said that there are two things you should never look into too closely: firstly, how sausages are made; secondly, how our tax laws operate. The question of what goes into our food is actually high on our minds now - and likewise we need to look deeply into the matter of public revenue - which is the metre of Ogilvie's radical and eternally relevant 'pastoral prose poem' - where we'll find some surprising answers to some of our deep social problems, not very least concerning our relationship with the land. Our target in publishing this book is *all* the people of Scotland (and beyond too) - for a democratic rebirth of our country long overdue.

This volume has been developed from DC MacDonald's 1891 *Birthright in Land* edition of Ogilvie's *anonymous* 1782 *Essay on the Right of Property in Land*. Because both Ogilvie's and MacDonald's original texts are quite lengthy, and since much of their peripheral content is of less immediate interest to readers today, we have edited them - especially Ogilvie's - with considerable freedom. Like an apple tree being pruned to bear fruit, we have cut out those dead sections of only historical interest; and too the rank growth, where his writing seemed very conditioned by the circumstances of his times (times dangerous to any *Revolutionist*); to let light into the heart of the tree, punctuation, a few archaic expressions, and some minor points of syntax have been modernised; and to rebalance the structure of the new-shaped tree, and preserve a proper flow in the much shortened text, we have reorganised the work and made good use of Ogilvie's own excellent *Synoptical Contents* and *Footnotes* to his *Essay*.

May the tree fruit heavily.

Foreword

Scotland
and the
Land
Question

by
Roger Sandilands

In his Biographical Notes on William Ogilvie, DC MacDonald describes the agitation in Scotland for land reform in its broad sense since the publication of Ogilvie's work. He discusses the nineteenth century schisms within the church over its relations with landed interests; Robert Burns's championing of an extension of the franchise beyond that same class; and the powerful appeal of the American economist and social reformer, Henry George, who campaigned throughout Britain and Ireland for the Single Tax on land values.

In the early years of the twentieth century Scottish followers of Henry George played a prominent role in the events that led to the constitutional crisis of 1909-10. In 1906 an influential delegation of 118 municipal bodies in Scotland persuaded the new Liberal Government to go forward with the valuation and local taxation of land values. The *Land Values (Scotland) Bill* was passed overwhelmingly in the House of Commons, but in 1907 and 1908 the bill was rejected or seriously mutilated in the House of Lords. When in 1909 the Lords also rejected Lloyd George's Finance Bill, which embodied provisions for the valuation of the land of the whole country, the government moved to repeal the Lords' right to interfere with Money Bills.

In 1931 Philip Snowden, the Labour Chancellor, presented proposals for the taxation of land values in his Finance Bill, but this measure was repealed following the fall of the Labour Government and pressure from the Conservatives in Ramsay MacDonald's Coalition Government.

Various attempts to tackle the land problem in the years since 1945, such as "betterment levies" and "development land charges" were misconceived, partly because they failed to distinguish the value of land from the value of improvements (buildings, etc). This has also been the case with the domestic and business rating systems. Reforms such as the poll tax were rightly derided and scrapped.   Agitation for reform in Scotland and elsewhere has recently sharpened the focus once more on to the land itself, in both rural and urban areas, as being the free gift of nature and our common birthright.   It is increasingly accepted that this birthright can only be returned to the people via the fiscal reforms proposed by visionaries such as William Ogilvie and Henry George.

"The Earth being the birthright of all mankind, its rental is the natural property of the people. . . . Every proprietor owes to the community a ground rent for the land which he holds".

Thomas Paine *Rights of Man*

Introduction

Our Birthright
in
Land

by
Peter Gibb

Man is of Earth. He *is* earth:
- from his coming, to his
returning - inseparable from it
in every sense, and unimaginable
without it. So it is, once again, that
we see things this way; and no longer do we
quite so *lord it up* on earth, as once we did, and as
Burns regretted to a mouse in November 1785 -

> " I'm truly sorry man's dominion,
> Has broken nature's social union,
> An' justifies that ill opinion,
>   Which makes thee startle
> At me, thy poor, earth-born companion,
>   An' fellow-mortal ! "

Perhaps our recent ecological "breakages" are passing into history. We do seem to be rediscovering, all over the world, the way of life that knows the essential truth: that all life is inextricably *linked,* bound together even, and that tied within that binding, tied up tight, is *Land* - the Earth itself. We come to see that each of us, as earth apart awhile, is personally bound tight to land. It feeds us and waters us, gives us air to breath, it clothes us and shelters us, and nourishes our souls, between delivering us and receiving us - and no amount of human "progress' will change that.

Now if there is a single right which can be said to belong to all men, then by this binding, it is *the right to his place on earth. This* is man's 'birthright in land'. Just as we each have an equal natural *tie* to our Mother Earth, so we each have an equal natural *right* by her. Just as we *are* one with the animals, the trees, the soil - our "earth-born companions" - so we realise that we *cannot* stand alone from that to which we are bound.

This new clear sighting of the great but suppressed truth of our human situation, can be found beginning to grow in almost every sphere of human life. But - unfortunately - only in *almost* every sphere, and the deficiency is critical; for it is in that most fundamental social matter - that of our society's instituted relationship with the land. There, such deep *ecological* awareness is nowhere to be seen. Indeed, we see that there is little correlation, hardly even superficially, between our existing major social structures and the structures required by the

Natural Laws of Earth. In our actual political arrangements today, where is our *true* connection to the land reflected in our modern social structures, institutions and laws? Where is the social embodiment of man's first birthright to be found today? The answer is, sad to say, in precious few places. As we - as individual men, women and children - come together in our societies, should not the social, political and economic structures we form, grow from and reflect the Nature-given orders and structures?

Axially defining our societies is the point of relationship between the community and the individual. In one direction, the relationship is manifested as the restrictions society places on the individual (that is, what it is permitted to take from him, such as consents to act, or social dues): simultaneously, in the other direction, the relationship is defined by the extent to which, *and means by which*, the individual empowers the social community and enables it to act. We see that the way society makes provision for its common expenses is a matter of central importance to it. In the arrangement adopted, potentially lies the key to embodying, at a deep level within our human social systems, that sought-for Natural Order.

However, here we encounter a paradox: for in actual fact, the reservoirs from which our public revenue is taken today are mainly *private* things, which we *tax* - (such as a man's labour, his savings, or his goods) - and have little or nothing to do with *community,* or the common gift of Nature. The fruits of our labour, the return on our savings, and the profit on our trading are all things which *by natural right* are fully ours to keep, since they are (in an undistorted economic system) truly the result of our own hands and minds at work. Society has no moral right, in normal circumstances, to demand any portion of these private things. So, what *can* society claim as its own?

Beyond the returns to labour, savings and trading of each individual man, there is a resource, a fund, which *can* be said to belong to all men equally: - that bestowed by his community-sharing in our common birthright of land - our common fund of Earth. The windfall gain which we presently permit a man to reap, with his exclusive possession of some part of our *common heritage* - can we honestly say that *that* is rightfully his, the result of his exertions?

So the question is this: how can man's commonality and individuality be simultaneously embodied, politically, in our society, to truly reflect the natural order? That is, how can *that which is common to us all* - the land - be *allowed* to all of us? - and how can we ensure the right of every individual to the full fruits of his labour on the earth? How *can* the birthright of each of us in Mother Earth be procured?

Should not the answer be:

FOR WHAT EACH MAN TAKES FROM THE COMMON FUND, HE SHALL PAY TO THE COMMUNITY *A RENT.*

For each plot of land or natural resource he holds, and so monopolises, each man shall pay to the community a rent. The rent shall be his payment for the right to the exclusive use of what he takes, and be due to those whose own rights are diminished by his taking - that is, the rest of mankind. Thereby shall each individual acknowledge his debt to Mother-Earth, and thereby shall the community be compensated for what, awhile, it has lent. So it is that *Community Ground Rent* gives us back our *birthright in land.*

The value of the land is the natural, *lawful,* proper, and in fact *practical* way, to raise public revenue, for a country being reborn in a new millenium.

" It is not enough that men should vote; it is not enough that they should be theoretically equal before the law. They must have liberty to avail themselves of the opportunities and means of life; they must stand on equal terms with reference to the bounty of nature.... This is the universal law. This is the lesson of the centuries. "

Henry George
Progress and Poverty

MacDonald's Preface

to

Ogilvie's *Essay on The Right of Property in Land*

- by **DC MacDonald** -

edited from the 1891 Edition of *Birthright in Land*
by **George Morton**.

Professor Ogilvie's *Essay* was written between 1776 and 1781, about a hundred years before Mr. Henry George wrote his *Progress and Poverty*. Both authors traversed the sorrowful jungle of Political Economy, and both discovered "the central truth". The independent testimony of the one is corroborated by the equally independent testimony of the other.

The same truth was revealed to John Locke between the years 1680 and 1690. And is there any doubt that it was seen by Moses, David, Socrates, and a host of prophets, poets, and philosophers, ages and ages before?

Do we not find the *Birthright of Man* stereotyped in the words "OUR FATHER"? The Faiths of the world, ancient and modern, whether considered natural or revealed, have all something in them, in common with genuine Christianity, which declares "*Equality of Rights*" between man and man.

"Whether", says Locke,* "we consider natural reason, which tells us that men, being once born, have a right to their preservation, and consequently to meat and drink and such other things as Nature affords for their subsistence, or 'revelation', which gives us an account of those grants God made of the world to Adam, and to Noah and his sons, it is very clear that God, as King David says (Psalm cxv., 16), '*hath given the earth to the children of men*', *given it to mankind in common.*

"As much land as a man tills, plants, improves, cultivates, and can use the product of, so much is his property. He, *by his labour*, does, as it were, enclose it from the common.

---

* *Essay on Civil Government.*

"God gave the world to men in common; but since He gave it for their benefit and the greatest conveniencies of life they were capable to draw from it, it cannot be supposed He meant it should always remain common and uncultivated. He gave it to the use of the industrious and rational *(and labour was to be his title to it);* not to the fancy or covetousness of the quarrelsome and contentious." And adds Professor Ogilvie: "Nor yet that it should be appropriated in such a manner as that, when not more than half cultivated, the farther cultivation and improvement should be stopped short, and the industry of millions willing to employ themselves in rendering the earth more fertile should be excluded from its proper field, and denied any parcel of the soil, on which it could be exercised, *with security of reaping its full produce and just reward*". "This title to an equal share of property in land" is declared by Professor Ogilvie to be a "BIRTHRIGHT *which every citizen still retains."* We shall see how far he advanced the question towards the standpoint of *Progress and Poverty.*

"The reform" - says Mr. Henry George - "I have proposed . . . is but the carrying out in letter and spirit of the truth enunciated in the Declaration of Independence - the 'self-evident' truth that is the heart and soul of the Declaration - 'That all men are created equal; that they are endowed by their

Creator with certain inalienable rights; that among them are life, liberty, and the pursuit of happiness!'

"These rights are denied when the *equal right to land* - on which and by which alone men can live - is denied. Equality of political rights will not compensate for the denial of the *equal right to the bounty of nature*. Political liberty when the *equal right to land* is denied, becomes, as population increases and invention goes on, starvation wages. This is the truth that we have ignored."

Such being the disease, what is the cure?

"It is necessary", says the Philosopher of Pittensear *, "that the object to be aimed at, and the means by which it may be obtained, should be again and again stated to the public in a variety of speculative views, and so rendered familiar to the understandings of men.

"Internal convulsions have arisen in many countries by which the decisive power of the state has been thrown, for a short while at least, into the hands of the collective body of the people. In these junctures they might have obtained *a just re-establishment of their natural rights to independence of cultivation and to property in land,* HAD THEY BEEN THEMSELVES AWARE OF THEIR TITLE TO SUCH RIGHTS, *and had there been any leaders prepared to direct*

---

* Ogilvie's ancestral home (see *MacDonald's Notes*). (Editor).

them *in the mode of stating their just claim, and supporting it with necessary firmness and becoming moderation.* Such was the revolution of 1688, at which time, surely, an article declarative of the NATURAL RIGHT OF PROPERTY IN LAND *might have been inserted in the Bill of Rights,* HAD THE PEOPLE AT LARGE BEEN BEFOREHAND TAUGHT TO UNDERSTAND THAT THEY WERE POSSESSED OF ANY SUCH CLAIM. *Such also was the late convulsion in America (1776), the favourable opportunities of which are not yet exhausted."*

It is interesting, as well as instructive, to notice the harmony that pervades the writings of these three Apostles of *Man's natural right to independence, his liberty to labour, and his Birthright in land.* John Locke stirred up the English Revolution of 1688, and in doing so he set a good example to the rest of the world, and raised his country to a glorious position among nations. We are only beginning to see this now. William Ogilvie was neither an idle spectator of the French Revolution of 1789, nor of the American Revolution of 1776. The man who regarded Revolutions as "favourable opportunities" for restoring the natural rights of mankind was, like John Locke, a practical philosopher. Mr. Henry George, as a political philosopher, is equally practical. He is a child of 1776, *in spirit and in truth!* He is a Lockist as regards the rights of labour - labour being the title and also the measure which alone can give to the individual an exclusive right of property in natural products. And he is an Ogilvist (which is only a logical development of the Lockist) as regards man's BIRTHRIGHT IN LAND - the basis of the SINGLE TAX *, and the door through which LABOUR may freely enter into possession, and enjoy, not a mere portion of its fruit, which some tyrant may set apart, but "its full produce and just reward".

Sad and strange to say, amidst our boasted civilisation, our profession of the Christian Faith, and our avowed belief in one impartial God, all knowledge in regard to the just and equal right of mankind to participate in the bounties of Nature, has hitherto been systematically boycotted. Until recently, the teacher of such principles was treated by *Law and Order* as a dangerous criminal. John Locke had to take shelter in Holland. William Ogilvie had to conceal himself *under a bushel* in Scotland. Many a noble son of Erin had to mount the gallows, while thousands suffered imprisonment, and millions were exiled from that unhappy country - a country which is still held like a mangled corpse in the crocodile jaws of commercial landlordism; and the monster will not let go its hold except on one

---

* The measure proposed in this book confusingly goes under several names today - The Single Tax, Land Value Taxation, Community Ground Rent, etc.. It is the last of these names however - COMMUNITY GROUND RENT - which most roundly and accurately describes, in modern terms, the nature of the reform we propose. (Editor).

condition, namely, to be allowed to gorge itself with British *blood*.

But why not utterly destroy this monster? What better service for our soldiers, blue-jackets, and policemen, than to employ themselves in destroying this common enemy of mankind? Parliament could do it, a royal warrant could do it, the sufferers have a right to do it, nay "every man hath a right" to destroy such monsters. "In transgressing the law of Nature", says John Locke, "the offender declares himself to live by another rule than that of reason and common equity, which is that measure God has set to the actions of men for their mutual security, and so he becomes dangerous to mankind; the tie which is to secure them from injury and violence being slighted and broken by him, which being a trespass against the whole species, and the peace and safety of it, provided for by the law of Nature, *every man upon this score*, by the right he hath to preserve mankind in general, may restrain, or where it is necessary, destroy things noxious to them, and so may bring such evil on any one who hath transgressed that law, as may make him repent the doing of it, and thereby deter him, and, by his example, others from doing the like mischief. And in this case, and upon this ground, *every man hath a right* to punish the offender, and be the executioner of the law of Nature."*

* **The renowned George Buchanan, the great-grand-father of British Liberty, puts it even stronger than this.**

25

The benevolent and magnanimous Professor Ogilvie had this passage before him when he wrote the first section of his Essay. In a foot-note he says: "It were unjust to censure the proprietors of land, however, for retaining and exercising, as they do, a right whose foundations have not been inquired into, and whose extent no one has yet controverted". Then he goes on to explain that ignorance is the root of the evil. There were many cases to which the modified doctrine of Professor Ogilvie would apply, e.g., the "humane landlords of England" of his own time, and some of the princes of ancient times, "who lived for the happiness of their people". The *commercial* landlord, who, he tells us in the same note, is "of all citizens the most pernicious", who burkes all inquiry into the foundations of his right, and who with the aid of lawyers and priests, fills the eyes of mankind with the dust of ignorance, he would leave to be dealt with in accordance with the principles approbated by Locke. We should not degenerate from these principles, and it is to be hoped that few readers will grudge the references here made to the once famous, but now forgotten - strangely forgotten - writings of one of the best of men, and one of the greatest philosophers the world ever produced, namely, John Locke.

Professor Ogilvie, who came after Locke, devotes himself in this treatise to one subject -

Birthright in land, it may be called. And the Author may be justly styled - *The Euclid of Land Law Reform.* He has left little or nothing unsolved in connection with the Land Question. He has given us a true base line - man's equal right to the raw material of the earth, to the air, to the water, to the rays of the sun, and all natural products - from which we can work out any problem, and by which we can test the "title and measure" of every man's property. Resting on this baseline - *man's natural rights* - he represents to us the perpendicular line of *man's right to labour,* "with security of reaping its full produce and just reward". Here we have the question in a nutshell. Take away the base line, and you have *no right to labour,* and *no produce or reward,* except what may be meted out by the usurper of your natural rights. You have to beg for leave to toil ! We thus see clearly how the robbery of labour may be prevented, and how impossible it is to put a stop to such robbery while the industrial classes neglect to claim and exercise their natural right - their right to an equal share in the earth, and all its natural products.

Strikes against low wages, high rents, unjust taxation, absurd conflicts between capital and labour, rebellions against this or that form of government, are futile skirmishes, and very frequently are of the suicidal cock-fighting order, at which the real enemy, elevated on a grand stand, simply laugh.

To contend successfully with these evils, society must learn to begin at the source thereof. While labourers are content to remain deprived of their natural rights, they must pay whatever ransom the brigands who have seized these rights choose to demand. Not only is industry robbed, taxed, and crippled, but the brigand, as dog-in-the-manger, very often puts an entire stop to it, and thus the happiness and comfort of millions of mankind, who are willing to work, are curtailed or wholly sacrificed, and misery and starvation reign instead. I am somewhat afraid to say hard things against brigandage. An institution that is still propped up by *Law and Order*, and supported (or winked at) on almost every hand by the avowed servants of Jesus Christ, must be touched with a "gentle hand". William Ogilvie has done so in the *Essay* now before us. Although a landlord himself, he did not disregard the truth, and it will be found that his pen was guided by an impartial and benevolent spirit.

It may be noted that the practical schemes propounded in the *Essay*, were intended only as "examples and beginnings of reformation", to use the author's own cautious language, and should be read as such, and in the light of the circumstances of his own time. Let the reader then peruse once more the close of the *Essay*, and ponder over the contents of the work, comparing his own ideas with those of the author, before coming to a hasty decision, and let no scheme for the happiness of mankind be rejected without at least attempting to substitute and promote a better one. The reader, in applying the author's principles to the present time, and having regard to present and future circumstances, will find that these principles are not of the hard and fast kind, but that   they are in accordance with Natural Law, and therefore may be accepted as eternal and universal in their application.

When a child is born, we recognise that it has a natural right to its mother's milk, and no one can deny that it has the same right to mother-earth. It is really its mother-earth, *plus* the dew and sunshine from heaven and a little labour, that supplies the milk and everything else required for its subsistence. The monster that would deprive a babe of its mother's milk, or would monopolise the breasts of several mothers, to the exclusion of several children, is not more deserving of being destroyed than the monster who seizes absolute possession of more than his share of the common mother of mankind, to the exclusion of his fellow-creatures.

Professor Ogilvie's *Essay* is a pastoral prose poem, through which we can realise this beautiful world, with its ample provision for satisfying man's instinctive and rational faculties of enjoyment. The

"Sovereign Power" from which all blessings flow is manifested as a wise, just, and impartial Creator, who invites us to make His laws our laws, and who in these latter days has delegated to us some wonderful powers, by which - with equality of rights and freedom of labour - the comforts of this life, and the products of the world, may be multiplied more than a thousand fold, *purposely* (shall we not say?) to increase the happiness and virtue of mankind.

The sun never sets, and when one group of workers are retiring to rest, on his "going down", another group are rising with him. Light and labour thus go their incessant rounds; and so it is with the seasons of seed-time and harvest - the eternal law of revolutions seems to regulate all things! Human speech, borne on the mysterious wings of thunder, revolves round the earth, and "man to man the world o'er" can hold instantaneous converse. Man himself revolves round the world, carried by his fire-souled amphibious steed from places where he lacks food, raiment, or enjoyment, to more hospitable regions. Or he can, with magic-like power, cause the superfluous granaries, larders, and wardrobes, to move from one side of the globe, to feed and clothe the hungry and naked on the other. Nature seems to have decreed - "There shall be no more famines!" But although the sun shines ceaselessly, and man's labour follows him steadily in his course, the flow of blessings which such evolutions naturally produce is polluted and diverted by the influence of landlordism, which, like a upas tree, poisons the surrounding atmosphere, spreads desolation in the country, and crowds the town with vice, want, disease, misery, and crime, far beyond the power of churches, charities, hospitals, divorce courts, and police courts to cure. There is only one cure - "Cut it down: why cumbereth it the ground?"

An Essay on the Right of Property in Land

by
William Ogilvie
of Pittensear

Professor of Humanity, and Lecturer on Political and
Natural History, Antiquities, Criticism, and Rhetoric,
in the University and King's College of Aberdeen

1782

edited by
Peter Gibb

(The municipal laws of every country are not only observed as a rule of conduct, but by the bulk of the people they are regarded as the standard of right and of wrong, in all matters to which their regulations are extended.

In this prejudice, however natural to the crowd, and however salutary it may be deemed, men of enlarged and inquisitive minds are bound by no ties to acquiesce without enquiry.

Property is one of the principal objects of municipal law, and that to which its regulations are applied with greatest efficacy and precision. With respect to property in movables, great uniformity takes place in the laws of almost all nations; they differ only as being more or less extended to details, comprehending the diversity of commercial transactions; and this branch of jurisprudence may be said to have almost attained to its ultimate maturity and perfection.

But with respect to property in land, different principles have been adopted by different nations in different ages; and there is no reason why that system which now prevails in Europe, and which is derived from an age not deserving to be extolled for legislative wisdom, or regard to the equal rights of men, should be supposed to excel any system that has taken place elsewhere, or to be in itself already advanced beyond the capacity of improvement, or the need of reformation.

So let it be considered what regulations a colony of men settling in a small island, just sufficient to furnish them subsistence, by the aid of high cultivation, would probably establish in order to render the independent subsistence of each individual secure, and to prevent any one, or a few, from engrossing the territory, or acquiring a greater share than might be consistent with the public good? Just such regulations respecting property in land, it would be in the interest of every state to establish at any period of its history.

It is to a free and speculative disquisition, concerning the foundation of this right of property in land, and concerning those modifications, by which it may be rendered in the highest degree beneficial to all ranks of men, that the author of these pages wishes to call the attention of the learned, the ingenious, and the friends of mankind.)

All Right

of property is founded either in occupancy or labour. The earth having been given to mankind in common occupancy, each individual seems to have by nature a right to possess and cultivate an equal share. This right is little different from that which he has to the free use of the open air and running water; though not so indispensably requisite at short intervals for his actual existence, it is not less essential to the welfare and right state of his life through all its progressive stages.

This right cannot be precluded by any possession of others and nor is it tacitly renounced by those who have had no opportunity of entering upon it. The opportunity of claiming this right ought to be reserved for every citizen. In many rude communities, this original right has been respected, and their public institutions accommodated to it; whenever conquests have taken place, this right has been commonly subverted and effaced; in the progress of commercial arts and refinements, it is suffered to fall into obscurity and neglect.

Speculative reasoners have con-founded this equal right with that which is founded in labour, and ascertained by mutual law. The right of a landholder to an extensive estate must be founded chiefly in labour, and the progress of cultivation gives an ascendant to the right of labour over that of general occupancy. But the public good requires that both should be respected and combined together, and although such combination is difficult, and has rarely been established for any length of time, it is the proper object of Agrarian laws, and effectual means of establishing it may be devised. Almost all of Agrarian laws have proceeded on the plan of restricting that *extent* of landed property which an individual may acquire, and not the nature and the force of that right with which the landholder is invested *. Thus endeavouring to establish an equality of fortune, they have been found impracticable, and, could they have been carried into execution, must have proved detrimental.

The value of an estate in land consists of three parts - the original, the improved, and the improvable valuet. That every man has a right to an equal share of

---

* *In Scotland today the same mistake is still being made!*

Under land monopoly, the "nature" of the landowner's 'right' - actually a 'privilege' - is society's *permission* to extract that rental payment which *by* right (birthright) is the community's own: and the "force" of this 'right' is delivered by *The Law of Rent and Depression of Wages* (see *Further Reading*). (Editor).

---

t The value of any piece of land can indeed be divided into the three separate parts Ogilvie proposes, viz: - the *original* value which the land might have borne in its 'natural state', prior to all development; the *improved* value which it has received from the improvements and developments bestowed upon it <u>by the proprietor</u> (buildings, cultivation, etc.); and the *improvable* value, which the land may still receive from *(possible* and *permitted)* future improvements and developments.

However, more recent thought recognises that for the purposes of site valuation for public revenue, we need distinguish only between the value of the unimproved site (which is entirely created by the presence and economic activity of the community, and therefore belongs to it) and the value of the improvements (which being created by the occupier belongs to him). (Editor).

the soil, in its original state, may be admitted to be a maxim of natural law. It is also a maxim of natural law, that everyone, by whose labour any portion of the soil has been rendered more fertile, has a right to the additional produce of that fertility, or to the value of it, and may transmit this right to other men. The original and the improvable value of a great estate still belong to the community, the improved alone to the landholder. *

If the original value of the soil be the joint property of the community, no scheme of taxation can be so equitable as a land-tax, by which alone the expenses of the state ought to be supported until the whole amount of that original value be exhausted; for the persons who have retained no portion of that public stock, but have suffered their shares to be deposited in the hands of the landholders, may be allowed to complain, if, before that fund is entirely applied to the public use, they are

* Although Ogilvie wrote his *Essay* essentially as an *agrarian-based* proposal for change, the land and tax reform he sets out addresses and resolves the key *urban* as well as rural problems in Scotland today. After all, it is in our cities, in the presence of concentrated populations, that by far the highest land values are found; and the effects of the *Community Ground Rent* measure would be just as beneficial here as in the country. (Editor).

subjected to taxes, imposed on any other kind of property, or any articles of consumption.

A just and exact valuation of landed property is the necessary basis of an equal land-tax. The original value is the proper subject of land-taxes: the improvable value may be separated from the improved, and ought to be still open to the claims of the community.

How preposterous, then, is the system of that country which maintains a civil and military establishment, by taxes of large amount, without the assistance of any land-tax at all ! - In that example may be perceived the true spirit of legislation as exercised by landholders alone. Property in land is the fittest subject of taxation; and could it be made to support the whole expense of the public, great advantages would arise to all orders of men. What then, it may be said, would not in that case the proprietors of stock in trade, in manufacture and arts, escape taxation, that is, the proprietors of one-half the national income? They would indeed, be so exempted;

and very justly, and very profitably for the State; for it accords with the best interests of the community, through successive generations, that active progressive industry should be exempted, if possible, from every public burden.

All property ought to be the reward of industry; all industry ought to be secure of its full reward; the exorbitant right of the landholders subverts both these maxims of good policy. It is the indirect influence of this monopoly which makes a poors-rate necessary; requires unnatural severity in penal laws; renders sumptuary laws unpolitical, and the improvement of machinery for facilitating labour unpopular, and perhaps pernicious. The oppressed state of the cultivators, being universal, has been regarded by themselves and others as necessary and irremediable. A sound policy respecting property in land is perhaps the greatest improvement that can be made in human affairs.

(And reformation in this important point is not to be despaired of; the establishment of property in land has changed, and may hereafter receive other innovations.)

The chief obstacle to

rapid improvement of agriculture is plainly that monopoly of land which resides in the proprietors, and which the commercial system of the present age has taught them to exercise with artful strictness, almost everywhere. Hereafter, perhaps, some fortunate nation will give the example of setting agriculture free from its fetters. A new emulation will then arise among the nations hastening to acquire that higher vigour and prosperity, which the emancipation of the most useful of all arts cannot fail to produce.

The actual state of Europe, with respect to property in land, is very different from what might be desired. That exclusive right to the improvable value of the soil which a few men, never in any country exceeding one hundredth part of the community, are permitted to engross, is a most oppressive privilege: by its operation, the happiness of mankind has been for ages more invaded and restrained, than by all the tyranny of kings, the imposture of priests, and the chicane of lawyers taken together, though these are supposed to be the greatest evils that afflict the societies of human kind.

The rent which may be taken for land ought to be submitted to regulations not less than the interest of money. Whatever good reasons may be given for restraining money-holders from taking too high interest, may with still greater force be applied to restraining proprietors of land from an abuse of their right. By exacting exorbitant rents, they exercise a most pernicious usury, and deprive industry that is actually exerted of its due reward. By granting only short leases, they stifle and prevent the exertion of that industry which is ready at all times to spring up, were the cultivation of the soil laid open upon equitable terms. It is of more importance to the community, that regulations should be imposed on the proprietors of land, than on the proprietors of money; for land is the principal stock of every nation, the principal subject of industry, and the use of which is most necessary for the happiness and due employment of every individual.

Nor is it less practicable to adapt regulations to the use of land than to the use of money, were the legislative body equally well inclined to impose salutary restrictions on both. The glaring abuses of the one might be as effectually prevented as those of the other; although the total exclusion of all manner of abuse from either is not to be looked for. But that class of men in whom the strength of every government resides, and the right of making or the power of influencing and controlling those who possess the right of making laws, have generally been borrowers of money and proprietors of land.

The monopoly of rude materials, indispensably requisite for carrying on any branch of industry, is far more pernicious than the monopoly of manufactured commodities ready for consumption. The monopoly possessed by landholders is of the first sort, and affects the prime material of the most essential industry.

The monopoly possessed by land-holders enables them to deprive the peasants not only of the due reward of industry exercised on the soil, but also of that which they may have opportunity of exercising in any other way, and on any other subject; and hence arises the most obvious interest of the landholder, in promoting manufactures.

That nation is greatly deceived and misled which bestows any encouragement on manufactures for exportation, or for any purpose but the necessary internal supply, until the great manufactures of grain and pasturage are carried to their utmost extent - it can never be in the interest of the community; it may be in that of the landholders, who desire indeed to be considered as the nation itself, or at least as being representatives of the nation, and having the same interest with the whole body of the people.

(When mention is made in political reasonings of the interest of any nation, and those circumstances, by which it is supposed to be injured or promoted, are canvassed, it is generally the interest of the landholders that is kept in view.)

In fact, however, their interest is, in some most important respects, directly opposite to that of the great body of the community, over whom they exercise an ill-regulated jurisdiction, together with an oppressive monopoly in the commerce of land to be hired for cultivation.

Property in Land, as at present established, is a monopoly of the most pernicious kind. The interest of landholders is substituted for that of the community; it ought to be the same, but it is not. The landholders of a nation levy the most oppressive of all taxes; they receive the most unmerited of all pensions: if tithes are oppressive to industry, rents capable of being raised from time to time are much more so.

Regarding the whole wealth of the community, as belonging of right to themselves, landholders stand foremost in opposing the imposition of exorbitant taxes by the State, forgetting the exorbitancy of that taxation which they themselves impose on the cultivators of the soil, and which the sovereign may in justice, and in the way of retaliation ought to, regulate and restrain.

They clamour aloud against pensions and sinecure places, bestowed by the sovereign, not adverting that their own large incomes are indeed pensions, and salaries of sinecure offices, which they derive from the partiality of municipal law in favour of that order of men by whom its regulations are virtually enacted.

There are districts in which the landholder's rents have been doubled within fifty years, in consequence of a branch of manufacture being introduced and flourishing, without any improvement in the mode of agriculture, or any considerable increase of the produce of the soil. Here, therefore, the landlords are great gainers, but by what industry or attention have they earned their profits? How have they contributed to the progress of this manufacture, unless by forbearing to obstruct it? And yet from the necessity under which the manufacturing poor lived, of resorting to these landholders to purchase from them the use of houses and land, for the residence of their families, they have been enabled to tax their humble industry at a very high rate, and to rob them of perhaps more than one-half of its reward.

Had the manufacturers of such districts possessed what every citizen seems entitled to have, a secure home of their own - had they enjoyed full property in their lands; would not then the reward of their industrious labour have remained entire in their own hands?

The encouragements granted to commerce and manufactures, and so universally extolled, seem merely schemes devised for employing the poor and finding subsistence for them, in that manner which may bring most immediate profit to the rich: and these methods are, if not deliberately, at least without inquiry, preferred to others, which might bring greater advantage to the body of the people directly, and ultimately even to the rich themselves.

What is it that in England restrains the early marriages of the poor and industrious classes of men? Alas! not the Marrlage Acl but a system of institutions more difficult to be reformed; establishing in a few hands that monopoly of land by which the improvable as well as the improved value of the soil is engrossed. It is this which chiefly occasions the difficulty of their finding early and comfortable settlements in life, and so prevents the consent of parents from being given before the legal age. It is this difficulty which even after that age is passed still withholds the consent of parents, restrains the inclinations of the parties themselves, and keeps so great a number of the lower classes unmarried to their thirtieth or fortieth years, perhaps for their whole lives.

What other reason can be given, than the influence of this monopoly, why in countries, for many ages not thinly inhabited, nor unacquainted with the arts of agriculture, so great a proportion of the soil should still remain barren, or at least far below that state of fertility, to which the judicious cultivation of independent occupiers could bring it?

While the cultivable lands remain locked up, as it were, under the present monopoly, any considerable increase of population, though it seems to add to the public strength, must have a pernicious influence on the relative interests of society, and the happiness of the greater number. By diminishing the wages of labour, it favours the rich, fosters their luxury, their vanity, their arrogance;   while on the other hand, it deprives the poor of some share of their just reward and necessary subsistence.

It were unjust to censure the proprietors of land, however, for retaining and exercising, as they do, a right whose foundations have not been inquired into, and whose extent no one has ever yet controverted.   It is the situation in which they find themselves placed that prompts their conduct;   nor can they readily conceive either the injustice or the detriment which the public suffers, by permitting such rights to be exercised.   On the other hand, the farmers and cultivators have no clear perception of the injustice and oppression which they suffer.   They feel indeed, and they complain, but do not understand, or dare not consider steadily, from what cause their grievances take their rise.   The oppressive rights of the one order, and the patient submission of the other, have grown up together insensibly from remote ages, in which the present state of human affairs could not have been foreseen.

The public good requires

that every individual should be excited to employ his industry in increasing the public stock, or to exert his talents in the public service, by the certainty of a due reward. Whoever enjoys any revenue, not proportioned to such industry or exertion of his own, or of his ancestors, is a freebooter, who has found means to cheat or to rob the public, and more especially the indigent of that district in which he lives. But the hereditary revenue of a great landholder is wholly independent of his industry, and secure from every danger that does not threaten the whole State. It increases also without any effort of his, and in proportion to the industry of those who cultivate the soil. In respect of their industry, therefore, it is a *taille* or progressive tax of the most pernicious nature; and in respect of the landholder himself, it is a premium given to idleness, an inducement to refrain from any active useful employment, and to withhold his talents, whatever they are, from the service of his country. If the circumstances in which he finds himself placed stimulate to any exertion at all, it is that insidious vigilance by which he himself is debased, and his dependents at once corrupted and oppressed.

It has been required of the magistrate that he should with the same assiduity apply rewards to virtue as punishment to vice. The part which he has to act in respect or these cases is very different. The natural sentiments of men are sufficient to repress smaller vices, and to encourage and reward great and striking virtues; but they are not vigorous enough to apply adequate punishment to great crimes, nor steady and uniform enough to secure due reward and regular encouragement to the common and ordinary virtues of human life.

Every man, and every order of men, have their peculiar commodity, which they bring to market for the service of the community, and for procuring the means of their own subsistence. It would be injustice and oppression, therefore, if any one order were to impose restrictions on any other, respecting the price they may demand for their peculiar commodity. This injustice, however, certain higher orders have attempted, though generally without success, to put in practice, on various occasions, against their inferiors - against hired servants, day labourers, journeymen, artists of various kinds - by prescribing limits to the wages they are allowed to ask or to receive.

These lower classes of citizens have only the labour of their hand for their commodity, and if any is more than another entitled to the privileges of a free and equal market, it is surely that which may be accounted more immediately the gift of nature to each.

The community has a right, no doubt, to restrain individuals from doing aught that may be pernicious or offensive: what right it can have to compel them to exert their industry for the public service, at a regulated price, may admit of question, excepting only those cases in which the safety of the state is brought into immediate and evident danger.

The indirect and remote influences of this monopoly are productive of many unnatural situations and many pernicious effects, which the skill of legislature is frequently employed in vain to redress. Were this monopoly anywhere removed, and the cultivation of the soil laid open upon reasonable terms, the lowest classes of men would not be destitute of wherewithal to maintain their decayed and infirm relations and neighbours. These charitable attentions, prompted by private affection, would be better discharged, than when they devolve on the public; and all that encouragement to idleness, that waste, and mismanagement, inseparable from poor rates, and other public institutions of this sort, would be spared.

Sumptuary laws have been frequently turned into ridicule, and not unjustly, as pretending to maintain an impracticable simplicity, and an unnecessary austerity of manners, among the great body of citizens; but they deserve a very different estimation, if considered as means of directing the public industry to those exertions which may be productive of the most extensive utility, and most valuable enjoyments to the community at large.

If those persons who spend their days in the manufactures of velvet and of lace could be induced to employ the same industry in raising grain, potatoes, and flax, would they not, by increasing the plenty of these necessary commodities, augment the real accommodation of a very numerous class of citizens? And would not the happiness thence arising more than compensate the scarcity of those frivolous refinements which may be required for the gratification of a few?

Why should it be necessary to restrain the industry which ministers to luxury? - Because the industry which is productive of essential plenty, is restrained.

In a country where the opportunities of exercising a natural employment, and finding an easy subsistence, were thus laid open to all, the temptations to theft and other violations of property would be very much diminished; nor could it be thought necessary to restrain such crimes by the unnatural severity of capital punishments.

In such a country no suspicion could arise, no surmise would be listened to, that the invention of machines for facilitating mechanical labour, could ever be pernicious to the common people, or adverse to the prosperity of the State.

Perhaps no government can claim to itself the praise of having attended with the same impartial care, to the interests of the lower, as of the higher classes of men. Those who are employed in cultivating the soil are placed below the regard of men in higher stations of public dignity and trust; nor are their sufferings and wrongs obtruded on every eye, like the misery of the begging poor. They themselves are not much accustomed to reflection; they submit in most countries to their hard fate, as to the laws of nature; nor are they skilled, when severer oppression has at any time awaked them to a sense of the injustice they suffer, in making known their feelings and their complaints to others. But if the intelligent, and the friends of mankind, will take some pains to inquire into the nature and extent of that oppression, under which the industrious groan, and the force of that exorbitant monopoly, from whence their grievances proceed; and if such men will employ the talents which nature has given them, in explaining these grievances, and the rigour of that monopoly, to the whole world, - Europe, enlightened Europe, will not be able to endure it much longer; and the subversion - nay, even the abatement - of this monopoly, with the abuses flowing from it, may well deserve to be accounted the best, and most valuable fruit of all her refinements and speculations.

If it be indeed possible to accomplish any great improvement in the state of human affairs, and to unite the essential equality of a rude state, with the order, refinements, and accommodations of cultivated ages, such improvement is not so likely to be brought about by any means, as by a just and enlightened policy respecting property in land. It is a subject intimately connected with the proper occupation and the comfortable subsistence of men; that is, with their virtue and their happiness. It is of a real substantial nature, on which the regulations of law may be made to operate with efficacy, and even with precision.

So powerful and salutary might the good effects of such an enlightened policy prove, so beneficial such a restoration of the claims of nature and the general birth rights of mankind, that it might alone suffice to renovate the strength of nations, exhausted by civil war, or by great and unsuccessful enterprises; and even in the most flourishing states, it might give rise to a new era of prosperity, surpassing all example, and all expectation that may reasonably be founded on any other means of improvement.

If we consider only how far the present state of property in land even in the best governed nations of Europe, is removed from that more equitable and advantageous system, we may almost be led to despair that any great progress can be made towards so remote an improvement, however much it may be desired. - On the other hand, the actual system of landed property in Europe is greatly changed from what it has formerly been. It has varied its form, with the prevailing character of successive ages; it has been accommodated to the rude simplicity of the more ancient times, to the feudal chivalry of the middle centuries, and to the increasing industry and cultivation of later more tranquil periods. It may now therefore be expected to receive a new modification, from the genius and maxims of a commercial age, to which it is too manifest that the latest establishment of landed property is by no means adapted, and that from this incongruity the most pernicious and most flagrant oppressions arise.

In the progress of the European system of landed property, the domestic, the feudal, and the commercial stages may be distinguished. In the first, the condition of the cultivator was secured from any great oppression, by the affectionate sympathy of the chief of his clan. In the second, it was still secured, and almost as effectually secured, by that need which his lord had of attachment, assistance, and support, in the frequent military enterprises and dangers in which he was engaged.

But in the commercial state there is no natural check which may establish the security of the cultivator; and his lord has hardly any obvious interest but to squeeze his industry as much as he can. It remains, therefore, for the legislatures of different countries to establish some control for protecting the essential interests of their common people. It is an object which deserves, and will reward, their care. In the dark and disorderly ages the oppression exercised over the cultivators could not be reduced to a system. Their landlords depended on their assistance and military services, and would not, therefore, hazard the diminution of their attachment. If at any time the landlord endeavoured to exact more than they were inclined to give, means of concealment and evasion were not wanting, by which his rapacity might be effectually eluded. But in the present times there is no reciprocal dependence, and all means of concealment and evasion are rendered by the order of our laws uncertain, or, indeed, vain.

In those disorderly times, whatever oppression, or chance of oppression, the cultivators of the field were exposed to, they saw their landlord exposed to others, perhaps greater and more frequent. There was common to both an uncertainty in the possession of their just rights; and to compensate this, a chance of obtaining by address somewhat beyond these rights. In the present times, these common chances are removed by the protection of established government. The rights of the higher orders are rendered perfectly secure, while those of the cultivators are laid open to their oppressions.

That free discussion which every subject now receives gives reason to hope that truth and utility will always triumph, however slowly. In politics, in agriculture, in commerce, many errors have been rectified in theory, and even the practice in some (though not in an equal degree) reformed. And shall it be reckoned, then, that in this, the most important of all temporal concerns to the greatest number of mankind, the most pernicious errors will be suffered to remain still unrefuted, or if not unrefuted still unreformed? It is not permitted to the friends of mankind to despair of aught which may tend to improve the general happiness of their species, any more than it is consistent with a magnanimous and genuine patriotism ever to despair of the safety of our country.

The collective body of the people, if at any time their power shall predominate, ought above all things to insist on a just regulation of property in land. It belongs to the community to establish rules by which this general right may become definite; but not to recognise such a right at all, not to have established any rules by which its claims may be ascertained and complied with, ought to be accounted essentially unjust. Means may certainly be discovered by which this general right of the community in the property of the soil may be clearly and practically ascertained.

Internal convulsions have arisen in many countries by which the decisive power of the State has been thrown, for a short while at least, into the hands of the collective body of the people. In these junctures they might have obtained a just re-establishment of their natural rights to independence of cultivation and to property in land, had they been themselves aware of their title to such rights, and had there been any leaders prepared to direct them in the mode of stating their just claim, and supporting it with necessary firmness and becoming moderation. Such was the revolution in 1688, at which time, surely, an article declarative of the natural right of property in land might have been inserted into the Bill of Rights, had the people at large been beforehand taught to understand that they were possessed of any such claim.

Under circumstances of public distress, even the higher and privileged ranks, awed into wisdom and humanity by the impending gloom, may be inclined to acquiesce in those regulations which tend to renovate the whole body of the State, though at the expense of diminishing in some degree the privileges and emoluments of their own order. They will consider that, unless the numbers, the industry, and the manly temper of the body of the people can be kept up, the fortune of the community must fall into continual and accelerated decline, and the privileges of every rank become insecure.

If, in the meantime, commerce is restrained and manufactures decline, let the cultivation of the soil be laid open, on reasonable terms and without delay, to the people thus deprived of their usual employment; such a resource would convert what they must account a misfortune into an opportunity of finding real and natural happiness.

What more effectual preparation can be made for the most vigorous defence of national liberty and independence, than to interest every individual citizen more immediately and directly in the welfare of his country, by giving him a share in the property of the soil, and training him to the use of arms for its defence. The former of these means of public security and defence is scarcely less requisite than the latter, the propriety of which is so generally understood.

As for the beneficial effects of such a statute, the candid and intelligent are requested to estimate in their own thoughts what these might prove in the district with which they are most particularly acquainted, and to consider whether it would not very much improve the condition and the prospects of the day labourer, the hired servant and the working manufacturer, without imposing on the established farmer or the landlord any unjust inconvenience? Whether it would not lessen the number of the indigent and the idle? After having made this estimate, let them consider what might have been the present state of that district had such a progressive Agrarian law been established there one hundred or even fifty years ago.

Various objects

have engaged the enthusiasm and excited the efforts of mankind in successive ages; schemes of conquest and settlement in one age; plans of civil and religious liberty in another; manufactures and commerce have now their turn; and perhaps in some not very distant age a just regulation of property in land may become the chief object of public spirited endeavours.

" Sic poscere fata, et reor, et si
quid veri mens augurat, opto. "

" Destiny is pointing us to it;
just as the birds in the air forecast,
so my own good reasoning tells me:
- *this is where we are going.* " *

---

* **Editor's translation.**

MacDonald's Biographical Notes

- by **DC MacDonald** -

edited from the 1891 Edition of *Birthright in Land*
by **George Morton**.

" See yonder poor, o'er labour'd wight,
So abject, mean, and vile,
Who begs a brother of the earth
To give him leave to toil;
And see his lordly *fellow-worm*
The poor petition spurn,
Unmindful tho' a weeping wife
And helpless offspring mourn. "

Robert Burns (says his brother Gilbert) "used to remark that he could not well conceive a more mortifying picture of human life than a man seeking work".

The life problem of the present day was clearly seen by Burns more than (two) hundred years ago, and he then pointed out that monopoly in land was the main source of human misery. He looked up to heaven and called as his witness -

> " THE SUN that overhangs yon moors,
> Out-spreading far and wide,
> Where hundreds labour to support
> A haughty lordling's pride ".

This miniature sketch was drawn from real life in his *own* country. Then, casting his eye beyond Scotland, and seeing landlordism rampant everywhere, he exclaimed -

> " But, oh! what crowds in ev'ry land,
> All wretched and forlorn ".

William Ogilvie, who was a compatriot of Burns, was born in the year 1736, and was thus twenty-three years older than Burns. The scenes from which Burns took his pictures must have been familiar to Ogilvie. Both were lovers of mankind, and there was a very strong mental affinity between them. Ogilvie was known as "the *gentleman* an' *scholar*", but never (except within a very limited circle) as a Land Law Reformer. This is a regretful circumstance. It is equally regretful that Burns is more known as "*a rhyming, ranting, roving billie*" than as a pioneer and great thinker, in regard to reforms for the benefit of mankind. If we study his epic of the "Twa Dogs", and his other writings in prose and verse relating to the Land Question and Man's Natural Rights, not only in the light of his own time, but also in the fierce light of the present day, we shall not be surprised at anything we find in Ogilvie's book. Even the seemingly modern-looking SINGLE TAX proposition, so clearly laid down by Ogilvie, will not astonish us. A look at the "Twa Dogs" shows us how *Caesar* was able to take a more advanced view of the situation than *Luath*. No doubt if William Ogilvie had been a poet instead of a philosopher, he would have expressed the thoughts he has given us in his book somewhat after the manner of the lines above-quoted.

Ogilvie and Burns saw eye to eye; but while Burns roused up his fellow-men from the gutter of serfdom, Ogilvie reasoned with them as to the causes which brought them to such a low condition, and also as to the means of reclaiming their natural rights. Ogilvie considered the whole question from a magnanimous, impartial, and truly scientific point of view. He pleaded for "free inquiry"; he sought after truth; he was not one of those rough-and-ready reformers who would simply say, "Abolish landlordism and all evils will vanish". No. He looked upon modern landlordism not as a cause but as an effect. The primary and fundamental cause of all the evils under which humanity suffers is traced by him to man's want of knowledge; and landlordism, with all its consequent evils, under which humanity groans, according to him, is directly owing to man's ignorance of his natural rights. It is this ignorance which begets slavish submission and breeds oppression. Ogilvie considered the situation logically. In his view IGNORANT HUMANITY MUST NEGLECT ITS RIGHTS, AND WITHOUT ITS RIGHTS CANNOT PERFORM ITS DUTIES. Rights and duties are co-relative. Ogilvie recognised this very old maxim of Natural Law. He saw the dishonest and absurd position which the landlords take up in every country. They first rob their fellow-men of their natural rights, and then they add insult to injury by accusing them of neglecting their duties. They call them poor and lazy, while at the same time they, as a rule, do no productive work themselves, and their whole wealth consists of property created by the labour of others. And these "freebooters", as Ogilvie calls them, are styled noblemen and gentlemen, and have arrogated to themselves the position of rulers and legislators in almost every country under heaven.

The people's ignorance of their natural rights is not only the primary, but it is also the sustaining, cause of landlordism. "Keep the people ignorant", says the tyrant to the priest, "and I'll keep them poor". In a note of Ogilvie's (omitted in this edition), reference is made to the ignorance of mankind thus: "In no article are they more ignorant than in respect to property in land, the established rules of which are in every country accounted permanent and immutable". The divine right of kings was until yesterday accepted as an article of faith, and we in Britain are still foolish enough to recognise grants of land signed by authority of *such* "divine" mandates! We do not now recognise the right of living monarchs to do such things, and yet we confirm, acknowledge, and practically homologate the musty parchments of King Tom, King Dick, and King Harry. "These be thy Gods, O Israel !" Their charters to the landlords, and the sub-charters by these landlords to others, including conveyances for borrowed money, are the *only* SACRED WRITS recognised in our Courts of *Law*. Mark the word "Law". Justice has to take a back seat whenever one of these SACRED WRITS is produced.

All titles to land are fetishes. In this country they are the fetishes of discarded and dead divinities. But such is the power of ignorance and superstition when established and maintained by LAW AND ORDER that these fetishes are held much more sacred now than in the so-called dark ages.

Our Judges are *specially paid,* and *sworn in,* not to question these SACRED WRITS. Our *National* Clergy are also *specially paid,* and *sworn in,* to instruct us about the SACREDNESS OF THESE WRITS. There is no water in the sea, and there is no bribery and corruption in the British Isles ! No ! We thank Heaven that we are not governed like other countries, where, as in America, bribery and corruption are *sometimes* investigated, and even exposed and punished. Our "permanent official" keeps all these things *square!* We British are a "Christian Nation"! If "agitators" would only keep away, the people would be contented and happy with their hope of glory in heaven. Why should *they* care about this earth - "this wicked world"? Why should they rebel against LAW AND ORDER? If they do not suffer oppression, misery, injustice, and poverty in this world, where do they expect to go when they die?

Somehow the rich do not act in accordance with a belief in our Creeds and Catechisms, but they nevertheless support by endowments and otherwise the establishment and spread of that *un*earthly Gospel *for the poor!* Ogilvie, by the way, makes a mild suggestion about an endowment for "the independence of the plough" - an endowment leading to "virtue and happiness *in this world".* He believed a little in that sort of thing.

Knowledge is no longer a *civil* crime. We can, for example, glance at the *style* of Fetish by which the land in Scotland *was seised,* and "by virtue of" which it is *now* held by the landlords. It is called an "Instrument of Sasine" or "Seizin", from the verb "seize". It begins with the words: "IN THE NAME OF GOD, AMEN !" and then narrates the *sacred* ceremony by which the landlords *required* "to complete their title" ! The sole purpose of this ceremony was to declare and promulgate the doctrine of the "divine right of landlords": a doctrine which was superinduced upon Feudalism by the aid of Priestcraft sometime during what we call the dark ages. And it is more than probable that it was during these dark ages that the same pernicious doctrine was ingrafted upon the faiths of *Christian* Europe. It was this that barred the doors and windows of men's minds against the smallest possible ray of knowledge "in respect to property in land", and hence the ignorance and superstition of "the bulk of mankind in every country", as Ogilvie truly states in his book. The doctrine of the "divine right of landlords", when fully established as an article of Faith in the minds of a people, notwithstanding its ridiculous monstrosity, its opposition to natural justice, and its poisonous effect on the natural feeling of patriotism and love of one's home, is as difficult to dislodge *as any other article of Faith.*

We get a very bright glimpse of Ogilvie's character where he deals with the "*divine* rights" by which Landlords and the Clergy levy rent and tithes. He puts these "*divine* rights" in one basket, and thus disposes of them: "The foundation of both rights, notwithstanding prejudices on either side, is precisely the same, viz., *the improvident regulations of municipal law*". Not only was he before his own time, but his views are about a century in advance of even the present day. But we can see this only after a careful study of his book, and by reading between the deep furrows which he has turned up for us. He knew from history that it is not by the sword that doctrines and beliefs are instilled into the minds of men. William the Conqueror introduced what is *called* Feudalism into England, *by the Pope's authority*, "IN THE NAME OF GOD, AMEN !" His successor, Henry II., introduced it into Ireland, *by the Pope's authority*, "IN THE NAME OF GOD, AMEN !" It was somehow smuggled into Scotland, whether by the Pope's express authority is not known, but that it was done "IN THE NAME OF GOD", and that the Priest said "Amen!" there cannot be a doubt; and on that blasphemous and fraudulent basis it now stands in Democratic, Presbyterian, and Protestant Scotland. It took many centuries to develop itself in the little country of the Scots. Strange to say, the overthrow of the Church of Rome, and the establishment of Protestantism at the *Reformation*, largely contributed to the establishing of the doctrine of the *divine right of landlords* in the Scottish mind *. The Landlords then made themselves the Patrons of the Religion of the people, and they not only "grabbed" all Church lands, but they also "grabbed" all the tithes, allowing only a pittance to the clergy.

We should not forget that all grants of land were originally given *in trust for the people,* and that the rents were originally levied for public purposes. The landlords were all public officers, but as they by degrees became sole legislators they legalised the embezzlement of all revenue from land. Then they taxed *the landless people.* They schemed many taxes. But the SINGLE TAX *restored* would put an end to all these!

---

* Note also that another *Reformation* - the Revolution of 1688 - was utilised in the same way by the *Divine* Party. The "False Argyll" reported that the people of Glencoe refused to discontinue the ancient Scottish tenure, and this was the *excuse* which led to the massacre in 1692. These little bits of history are carefully slipped over by the majority of our so-called historians, like all other facts relating to the people's right to the land. But the most extraordinary thing connected with Scotland and the *divine right of landlords* is to be met with in connection with the last *Reformation* - the "Disruption" of 1843, when the *Free Church* was instituted. A very large section of the Scottish people, and *all* the Highlanders, then revolted in regard to the land-lord's *divine right of property in Church Patronage.* The "Auld Kirk" was deserted. But the clergy of the New (Free) Church have done more in the Highlands of Scotland towards getting the doctrine of the *divine right of landlords* TO THE LAND, *into the minds* of the people, than had been done by *all other forms of Priestcraft,* from William the Conqueror's time to 1843. This strange fact, and its sad consequences, will be referred to further on. If these "dissidents" had taken up Ogilvie's cue of favouring a just and independent land reform in 1843, the *Free Church* and Scotland would be in a better position to-day.

It is the right, the duty, and the *interest* of every citizen to demand the just occupation and taxation of the land, and to insist that the dishonest and criminal administration of private *unlimited* ownership of land should no longer be tolerated.

The declared object of Ogilvie's book*, is to show how "property in land might be rendered more beneficial to the lower ranks of mankind". A somewhat dark, unwritten page in British history relates the disgraceful fact that both author and book were boycotted, and that up to this time (1889!) the lower ranks of mankind in England, Scotland, Wales, Ireland, and the British Colonies never heard that such a man lived, far less that he left them such a legacy. "The worthy and humane English landholders", whom he appointed * as his literary trustees, evidently neglected their duties to the intended beneficiaries. We may guess that the French Revolution gave these worthies a scare, and that the author was regarded in those days as rather a dangerous man. It would be said that he was dangerous to the community, dangerous to society, and dangerous of course to the NATION - *that is,* the landholders. He himself anticipated all that: see his *Essay* (p.46) as to what constitutes "any nation"! But I must leave the reader to find out for himself to what extent the work is based upon truth

---

* As stated in the *Essay's* original title and introduction. (Editor).

and justice, and how much the author was prompted by love for mankind as the ruling spirit or chief feature of his character.

The facts known about Ogilvie's life are exceedingly scanty, and would of themselves be of little importance; but when considered along with the conception we form of the man as displayed on every page of his book, the smallest scrap of authentic information will in these days be of some interest, not only to "men of enlarged and inquisitive minds", but also to readers in general. It is in the book, however, and in the book alone, that we meet face to face with the author. Ogilvie instilled his soul into it, and he left us evidence that it was the chief aim of his life. We, therefore, should as soon think of separating the man Isaiah from the Book of Isaiah, as we should of separating the man Ogilvie from the book of Ogilvie.

He is buried in the south transept of the Cathedral in Old Aberdeen. A small tablet in the wall describes him as "William Ogilvie, Esquire of Pittensear, in the County of Moray, and Professor of Humanity in the University and King's College, Aberdeen, who died on the 14th February 1819, aged 83 years". This tablet is enough to make us think that we are unearthing the wrong man. Here we have a landlord who is also a University Professor.

We know what landlords in general are, and we also know what no less an authority than Adam Smith said about Universities - that they were "the sanctuaries in which exploded systems and obsolete prejudices found shelter and protection after they had been hunted out of every other corner of the world". When, however, we find Ogilvie hurling this very quotation at his fellow-professors in connection with a University reform he advocated in 1786, and when we also discover that his views and proposals regarding such reform were fully as advanced as his schemes for dealing with property in land, the doubts suggested by the tablet become less formidable.

Ogilvie finished his *Essay* in 1781, eight years before the French Revolution broke out. He was "well aware that great changes suddenly accomplished are always pregnant with danger", and he said so, as a warning to the "friends of mankind". He studied the question in his own careful way beforehand, and foretold what would happen. But the oppressors and their tools turned a deaf ear to all warnings. Every page of his book is full of humane wisdom, and while he manifests great sympathy for the oppressed, his feelings regarding the oppressors are mingled with a kind of sympathetic pity, rather than pure indignation. His very strong sense of justice was balanced and kept within reasonable bounds by his knowledge of the world's history and his study of the Laws of Nature, and especially his study of human nature.

The present state of "Enlightened Europe", with its growing evil of military despotism, its heaps of wealth in the hands of a limited number of individuals or syndicates, the terrible increase of public debts, the growing struggle for existence, the appearance of old-world evils in new countries, all mainly due to the general neglect of the natural rights of mankind in this matter of property in land, must suggest to the dullest reader that we are still far from realising what the author looked forward to in the last paragraph of his book, and what his compatriot Burns prayed for, and prophesied thus: -

" THEN LET US PRAY THAT COME IT MAY
       (AS COME IT WILL FOR A' THAT),
THAT MAN TO MAN, THE WARLD O'ER,
       SHALL BROTHERS BE FOR A' THAT ".

It is impossible to say that such a lover of mankind as William Ogilvie kept himself willingly behind the scenes during his whole life. It is perhaps more correct to say that he did not; and that it is only now that the curtain of error and prejudice is being raised. When we know that even Burns's bright star was almost totally obscured in those dark days, what chance could the like of Ogilvie have had? Burns died of hard work and starvation. He carried about with him a broken heart and a shattered frame from the time he was a mere boy, when he was compelled to overwork himself at the plough, at the scythe, and at the flail, trying to assist his struggling parents to pay an impossible rent. He saw his father murdered - sacrificed on the altar of landlordism, in "Christian", "Bible-loving", "pious", but, *then*, laird-worshipping Scotland. Burns never recovered from the effects of this landlord oppression to which he was subjected in his youth, and especially the shock of his father's death. Scenes like the following picture of wretched Scotland in those days may have prompted Ogilvie to write his book. It is the "gentleman an' scholar" speaking in the "Twa Dogs": -

> " L__d, man, our gentry care as little
> For *delvers*, *ditchers*, an' sic cattle;
> They gang as saucy by poor folk
> As I wad by a stinkin' brock.
> I've notic'd, on our Laird's *court-day*,
> An' mony a time my heart's been wae,
> Poor *tenant bodies*, scant o' cash,
> How they maun thole a *factor's* snash;
> He'll stamp an' threaten, curse an swear,
> He'll *apprehend* them, *poind* their gear;
> While they maun stan', wi' aspect humble,
> An' hear it a', an' fear an' tremble! "

It was in 1775, when Burns was 16 years of age, that his soul was impressed by this painful experience. In his autobiography he says: "My father's generous master*died; the farm proved a ruinous bargain; and, to clench the misfortune, we fell into the hands of a factor who sat for the picture I have drawn of one in my tale of 'The Twa Dogs'. There was a freedom from his lease in two years; we retrenched our expenses and lived very poorly. A novel writer might have viewed these scenes with satisfaction; but so did not I. My indignation yet boils at the recollection of the scoundrel factor's insolent, threatening letters, which used to set us all in tears." These words were penned in August 1787, and the scene of 1775 was still burning in the soul of the poet. In the interval Adam Smith published his great work, *The Wealth of Nations*, in 1776, and Ogilvie's book followed. But we should also notice that another Scotsman was before them, namely, Thomas Spence, who, on 8th November 1775, delivered a lecture before the Philosophical Society of Newcastle, in which he declared, in the strongest terms, that all men "have as equal and just a property in land as they have in liberty, air, or the light and heat of the sun"; and for the printing of that lecture, the Newcastle philosophers, he tells us, "did him the honour to expel him" from their Society.

---

* This is the language of serfdom. In the Court of Session
(*ultra vires*), *Act of Sederunt* of 1756, anent Evictions, the terms used
are "masters and tenants". Thus qualified, the word "tenants" legally
meant *serfs*. The *bond* was called "a lease". Mark the words "freedom
from his lease". The "tenant-at-will" was a mere slave.

Burns and Spence belonged to what the world calls the *lower orders*, whereas William Ogilvie of Pittensear was a born and bred patrician, and was lineally descended from Gillecrist, who was the last *Maor Mor* of Angus, one of the seven provinces of Celtic Scotland. Ogilvie, like his more distinguished compatriot, Burns, was by birth and lineage an anti-Whig, and, as a man, he must have despised the wirepulling *Scotch* Whigs of his time as *"but a pack o' traitor louns"!* He was the only son of James Ogilvie of Pittensear, Morayshire, and of Marjory Steuart of Tannachy, in the neighbouring county of Banff. There is no authentic account of his boyhood, but it may be assumed that he was brought up in the little mansion-house of Pittensear, and that he attended the Grammar School at the county town of Elgin until he left home for College. Pittensear House is within five miles of Elgin.

At the age of nineteen he entered King's College, Aberdeen, as third bursar of his year, 1755-56. He graduated in 1759, and was then appointed Master of the Grammar School at Cullen. He remained in Cullen only for a year. We find him attending the Glasgow University during the winter session of 1760-61, and the Edinburgh University during the winter session of 1761-62. In Glasgow, he studied under Dr. Joseph Black, at the very time that eminent chemist was expounding his great discoveries regarding "Latent Heat and Specific Heat", and when James Watt was busy in his little workshop in the College buildings making *his great discoveries.* We may safely conjecture that Ogilvie paid many visits to that little shop along with Joseph Black and other frequenters, and we may put it down as a certainty that he did not miss the lectures of Adam Smith, who then occupied the Chair of Moral Philosophy. Among the eminent professors in Edinburgh whose lectures he presumably attended were Dr. Blair, Professor of Rhetoric, author of *Lectures on Belles Lettres;* Dr. Adam Ferguson, then Professor of Natural Philosophy, afterwards of Moral Philosophy, author of an *Essay on the History of Civil Society,* and a *History of the Progress and Termination of the Roman Republic;* and Dr. Cullen, Professor of Chemistry, famous for being the first in Britain to teach chemistry as a science.

Ogilvie was, on the 29th of November 1761, appointed an Assistant Professor of Philosophy in King's College, Aberdeen, "upon the assurance which the members (of the College) gave Lord Deskfoord that he should be chosen into the first vacant office that might happen of a Regent's place". The first vacancy occurred on the 16th of October 1764, when Thomas Reid, Regent and Professor of Philosophy, resigned.

Ogilvie did not begin to teach as a "Professor of Philosophy" in King's College until November 1762, when an engagement under which he was at the time of his appointment, as tutor to a Mr. Graeme, expired. It was also his own desire "not to leave Edinburgh" during the winter of 1761-62; "and, further", says Lord Deskfoord, "he apprehends that his attending the most eminent professors at Edinburgh for this session may qualify him better than he is at present for teaching afterwards in the College of Aberdeen".

It was still the old system of teaching in Aberdeen, and Ogilvie, as a "Professor of Philosophy", was expected to teach the whole circle of the sciences - "the sciences of quantity, of matter, and of mind". There were no separate Professors of Mathematics; of Natural Philosophy, Natural History, Chemistry, or Botany; of Logic or Moral Philosophy, in King's College in those days. The three Regents (who were generally styled "Professors of Philosophy") were expected to teach all these subjects, and also to give lectures on Geology, Meteorology, Astronomy, Natural Theology, Rhetoric, Economics, Jurisprudence, and Politics. The students, under the old system, did not change from one professor to another; but each Regent, in his turn, took the second year's class, and carried on the same students continuously for three years.

In 1765, the year after Ogilvie's appointment as full Regent, he exchanged offices with the Professor of Humanity. This gave him greater scope, as all the students attended the Humanity Class. On the 23rd of September 1765, the Masters approved of the proposed exchange, and from this date Professor Ogilvie taught the Humanity Class until 1817, when, *at his own request*, an assistant and successor was appointed. "For upwards of half-a-century Prof. Ogilvie was perhaps the most energetic member of Senatus, his decidedly progressive views bringing him not unfrequently into conflict with his more conservative colleagues. The pages of the College Minutes during his incumbency bristle with protests against, and reasons of dissent from, the decision of the majority." *

During the period from April 1759, to November 1762, we may take it for granted that Ogilvie lost no opportunity of acquiring such knowledge and accomplishments as he deemed a professor in those days should possess. Besides his attendance at the Glasgow and Edinburgh Universities, it is most probable that he visited England and the Continent, and made himself acquainted with the various systems of teaching carried on in the principal seats of learning in Europe. He was travelling tutor and

---

* **Note by Mr P J Anderson, Secretary to the NEW SPALDING CLUB, in** *Scottish Notes and Queries* **for June, 1889.**

companion to Alexander, 4th Duke of Gordon, and the fact of the Duke's having visited the Continent is well known, but there is an uncertainty as to the precise date. It may be mentioned that Adam Smith resigned his professorship in Glasgow about the year 1763, on account of his engagement as travelling tutor and companion to Henry, 3rd Duke of Buccleuch, and as Gordon was Buccleuch's senior by three years, it is not improbable that Gordon and Ogilvie visited the Continent about the years I760-6I, or '62. But be this as it may, the reader will not fail to see from *The Right of Property in Land* that its author not only visited the Continent of Europe, but that he also made a special study of the condition of its people about the latter half of the eighteenth century. He saw the French Revolution coming, and the causes leading up to it: "The widow is gathering nettles for her children's dinner; a perfumed seigneur, delicately lounging in the Œil de Bœuf, hath an alchemy whereby he will extract from her the third nettle, and call it rent." *

    In Ogilvie's time landlordism was most rampant in his own country. He witnessed the passing of the Act 1747, by which military tenure in all Scotland, and the ancient clan tenure in the Highlands, were respectively abolished; and he must have

---

* **Carlyle's** *Past and Present,* **inspired by Byron, see AGE OF BRONZE XIV. "The grand agrarian alchemy, high** *rent.***"**

noticed with much pain the establishment of serfdom which followed. He saw oppression, poverty, and misery introduced by "THE REIGN OF LAW AND ORDER" which then prevailed; and, worst of all, he saw the Scotch peasantry not only submitting to the lawless oppression of the tyrant, but also cringing before the very parasites of squirearchy.

The soul of Justice as well as the soul of Freedom had fled from Scotland in Ogilvie's time, and he himself was compelled to live as a sort of exile *in his own country!* Reader, do not, therefore, wonder that in his book on the Land Question, while he referred (in his original unedited *Essay*) to almost every country in the world, he was obliged to draw his pen through Scotland and its people. He refers to England like an Englishman, to Ireland like an Irishman, and he even stands up as a patriot for Orissa and Bengal; but he draws the line sharp and clear when we find him referring to England, Bengal, Egypt, Ireland, "or the northern counties of England"! On consulting his compatriot and contemporary, Burns, I am satisfied that the omission of all reference to Scotland proceeded from sheer disgust at the utterly slavish condition of his countrymen at the time he wrote. His only hope lay in the adoption by Scotland of the *English* Revolution principles of 1688. If the Scots, the Irish, and also the French had joined in that Revolution and assisted the English in selecting a MAN, instead of a Prince, as chief trustee of those rights and liberties which the Revolution gave birth to, it would have been better for all. Peace and Reform, instead of war and tyranny, would have followed. It was the Prince of Orange that, in 1692, granted the warrant for the Massacre of Glencoe. He, and the intriguers who procured, and the savages who executed, the royal mandate, ought to have been *suspended*. Scotland was evidently denied *English* justice as well as *English* liberty. The Revolutions of 1715 and 1745 were natural consequences. Some time after 1745, Scotland was made a recruiting ground for an army and a navy used in maintaining the slave trade, and also in fighting against American Independence. Add to this the effect of internal strife between creeds and factions, a corrupt executive government, not to mention landlord oppression, and the words knavery and slavery will suggest themselves as applicable to the condition of the inhabitants of Scotland then. In Ogilvie's time many thousands *were forced* to emigrate "in search of their natural rights".

Thomas Muir, Younger of Huntershill, a member of the Scottish Bar, but better known as the "Political Martyr of 1793", was on the 30th August of that year tried before the High Court at Edinburgh, for the *crime* of having attended one or two public meetings in connection with the extension of the franchise, *which was then strictly limited to landlords*. For this heinous *crime* he was sentenced to fourteen years transportation - *to death*, it may be said, for the sentence directly led to a premature grave. The trial was conducted in the most insulting way possible, not to speak of the treasonable manner in which a landlord judge and jury (a servile Bar aiding and abetting) trampled the British Constitution under foot. As for justice, there was not even the *form* of it observed. The jury was a packed one. It consisted of nine landlords, one bookseller, two bankers, and three Edinburgh merchants; and when one of these merchants (Mr. John Horner) was passing the bench to get into the box, Lord Braxfield, in a whisper, addressed him thus: "Come awa, Maister Horner, come awa, and help us to hang ane o' thae damned scoundrels". The same judge was in the habit of saying, when any legal difficulty occurred in framing libels against such *criminals* as Thomas Muir, William Ogilvie, or Robert Burns: "Let them bring me prisoners and I'll find them law".

I should have preferred not to soil these pages with the name of Braxfield, but as I believe he betrayed his knowledge of Ogilvie's book, by making the worst possible use of it at Muir's trial, I am disposed to return good for evil by doing his Lordship the honour of giving a quotation from his speech on that occasion, and placing it alongside Ogilvie as a first-rate argument in favour of the SINGLE TAX.

Braxfield.

" A government in every country should be just like a corporation, and in this country it is made up of THE LANDED INTEREST, WHICH ALONE HAS A RIGHT TO BE REPRESENTED. AS FOR THE RABBLE, WHO HAVE NOTHING BUT PERSONAL PROPERTY, WHAT HOLD HAS THE **NATION** OF THEM? WHAT SECURITY FOR THE PAYMENT OF THEIR TAXES? THEY MAY PACK UP ALL THEIR PROPERTY ON THEIR BACKS AND LEAVE THE COUNTRY IN THE TWINKLING OF AN EYE, **BUT LANDED PROPERTY CANNOT BE REMOVED**. " - *The Martyrs of Reform in Scotland,* by A.H. MILLER.

Ogilvie.

" It is indeed *the landed property of the nation that is ultimately and solely engaged for all national debts; every other species of property may be concealed, transferred, or withdrawn, when the demand for payment is apprehended.* It is therefore to be wished, for the security of public credit . . . that property in land were exceedingly divided; so that every person had a share. . . . It becomes even the interest of the great landholders, that such a distribution of property in land should take place . . . . *So that every member (of society) may be rendered responsible for the public debt.* " [from a section of Ogilvie's *Essay* omitted in this edition.]

It is interesting to note that Burns wrote his Revolution song, "Scots! wha hae wi' Wallace bled", in September 1793, immediately after the sentence of Thomas Muir. On the 30th of the same month he presented to the Subscription Library of Dumfries a copy of *De Lolme on the British Constitution*, on which he inscribed the following words: "Mr. Burns presents this book to the Library, and begs they will take it as a creed of British Liberty, until they find a better. - R.B.". The significance of this present at the time he composed "Scots! wha hae", and when Thomas Muir and other worthy "sons" were in "chains", will be clearly understood from the following passage which DE LOLME quotes, in Chapter XIV. of his book, from Blackstone's Commentaries on the Law of England (Book I., Cap.I.), in reference to the lawfulness of Revolution, whenever the rights of the people are trampled upon.

Blackstone says: - "And lastly, to vindicate those rights, when actually violated or attacked, the subjects of England are entitled, in the first place, to the regular administration and free course of justice in the courts of law; next, to the right of petitioning the King and Parliament for redress of grievances; and lastly, TO THE RIGHT OF HAVING AND USING ARMS FOR SELF-PRESERVATION AND DEFENCE".

These were the principles of the English Revolution settlement of 1688, and upon which the British Constitution was based. Considering the very complete knowledge of the *legal* rights of British citizens, that Burns possessed through his study of De Lolme's admirable book, and his own very keen sense of man's natural rights, together with his extreme abhorrence at all forms of injustice, and especially when such injustice is perpetrated in the name of LAW AND ORDER, we need not waste much time in speculating as to how he felt on hearing the result of Thomas Muir's trial. It is enough to say that he there and then composed a war song for Scotland - a *Marseillaise!*

He himself has not left us in any doubt. Here are his words: - "I showed the air ('Hey tuttie taitie') to Urbani *, who was highly pleased with it, and begged me to make soft verses to it; but I had no idea of giving myself any trouble on the subject till the accidental recollection of that glorious struggle for freedom, associated with the glowing ideas of some other struggles of the same nature, *not quite so ancient,* roused my

---

* **Pietro Urbani, an Italian musician, who met Burns at St. Mary's Isle, the seat of Lord Selkirk, on 31st July 1793, the day before Burns's ride with Mr. Syme "in the middle of tempests over the wildest Galloway moor", when "Scots! wha hae" was *thought*, through the suppression of the correct date, to have been composed.**

rhyming mania" *.   Mark the words, *not quite so ancient*, which Burns himself puts in italics. Then let us ask ourselves whether this soul-stirring Ode was not a real cry to arms against Braxfield and Company? Let us look at the Ode itself and the short prayer to God with which it concludes, and ask ourselves whether Burns had the English Edward or the Scotch landlords in his mind's eye at the time he wrote it, and let us not forget that he thoroughly approved of adopting the *English* Constitution in Scotland, and that he by no means wished to revive old national feuds.

---

*   Letter, sending "Scots! wha hae", to Mr. Thomson, dated "September, 1793", received in Edinburgh on the 3rd or 4th, and replied to on the 5th.   Referring to the old air "Hey, tuttie, taitie", Burns says, "There is a tradition, which I have met with in many places in Scotland - that it was Robert Bruce's march at the battle of Bannockburn.   This thought, *in my yesternight's evening walk*, warmed me to a pitch of enthusiasm on the theme of liberty and independence, which I threw into a kind of Scottish ode fitted to the air, that one might suppose to be the gallant royal Scot's address to his heroic followers on that eventful morning." The words "my yesternight's evening walk", were changed by Dr. Currie into "my solitary wanderings", and this error was not discovered until shortly before Mr. Robert Chambers of Edinburgh published his edition of Burn's works in 1857.   Dr. Currie's edition was published specially for behoof of Burns's widow and children, and many things were suppressed through fear of being boycotted by the "classes". It will be seen that the news of the brutal sentence passed on Thomas Muir would reach Dumfries, in those days, on 31st August or 1st September 1793. The "yesternight's evening walk" which produced "Scots wha hae" must have been on Sunday the 1st or Monday the 2nd, and Burns must have despatched it on the 2nd or 3rd, more probably the 2nd, as Mr Thomson says he read it to some friends *in Edinburgh* on the 4th.

   Mr. Thomson wanted Burns to alter this ode, but Burns refused. He writes on 15th September, in reply to Mr. Thomson, stating that the proposed alterations would "make it tame". "I have (he said) scrutinised it over and over; and to the world, some way or other, it shall go as it is." The world's verdict is in favour of the poet. "So long (says Carlyle) as there is warm blood in the heart of Scotchman or man, it will move in fierce thrills under this war ode; the best we believe that was ever written by any pen."

" By Oppression's woes and pains!
By your Sons in servile chains!
We will drain our dearest veins,
            But they *shall* be free!
Lay the proud Usurpers low!
Tyrants fall in every foe!
LIBERTY'S in every blow! -
            Let us Do - or Die !!! "

" So may God ever defend the cause of
Truth and Liberty as He did that day!
                        Amen!
                                    - R.B. "

Here we have Burns at bay. There were then only 2652 Parliamentary voters in Scotland *. This number included all the landed gentry and their faggots. These were undoubtedly the "proud usurpers" who caused the "oppressions, woes, and pains", referred to by our patriot bard.

We must not forget another circumstance. When Thomas Muir was apprehended on 2nd January 1793, Burns was at that very time being court-marshalled by the Board of Excise for a similar *crime!* On 5th January, in a letter to his

---

* **These were the NATION *à la* Braxfield!**

friend Mrs. Dunlop, he says: "The political blast that threatened my welfare is overblown". On the same day he writes to Mr. Graham of Fintry, who was mainly instrumental in shielding him from that "blast", making the solemn promise - "henceforth I seal my lips".

What happened in the interval between the 5th of January and September 1793, the reader already knows. He also knows that Burns broke his vow. The soul of Burns could not be caged. The theme of LIBERTY was a part of it, and death only could close those lips. He was not a coward. The man who wrote -

> " Wha will be a traitor knave?
> Wha can fill a coward's grave?
> Wha sae base as be a slave?
> Let him turn and flee! "

- in September 1793, *meant what he said*. He meant Revolution. We must not go about the bush in stating this. To do so would imply a cowardly slander on Burns. Alas! Caledonia -

> " Where is *thy* soul of freedom fled? "

For nine weary months Burns waits in vain for a response to his song of war: Scotland was no longer *the land of the free*. To the eye of Burns it was now the very burying ground of Liberty. The great soul of the poet is then borne away on its own soliloquy: -

" Swiftly seek, on clanging wings,
　　Other lakes and other springs;
And the foe you cannot brave,
　　Scorn at least to be its slave. "

TO HIS COUNTRYMEN HE BIDS THIS FAREWELL: -

" Avaunt! thou caitiff servile, base,
　　That tremblest at a despot's nod,
Yet, crouching under the iron rod,
　　Canst laud the arm that struck the
　　　　　　　　　　insulting blow!
Art thou of Man's imperial line?
Dost boast that countenance divine?
　　Each skulking feature answers, No! "

AND HE HAILS THE AMERICANS THUS: -

" But come, ye sons of Liberty,
　　Columbia's offspring, brave as free,
In danger's hour still flaming in the van,
　　Ye KNOW, and dare maintain,
　　　　　　the ROYALTY OF MAN ! "

These lines are quoted from the Ode to LIBERTY, a stanza of which was sent by the poet to Mrs. Dunlop in June 1794. The remainder was *im*MUIRED until 1872 (!), when Mr. Robert Clarke of Cincinnati purchased the original manuscript in London, and to him the world is indebted for its first publication. This Ode forms a key to the real intention, feeling, and purpose of "Scots! wha hae". They should be read together. And if the reader wants to see further into the soul of Burns, in regard to the theme of LIBERTY, from and after September 1793, he will find Scotland dealt with precisely as in Ogilvie's book. His "TREE OF LIBERTY", composed in 1794 (but boycotted until 1838)*, ends with these lines: -

" Syne let us pray, AULD ENGLAND may
   Sure plant this far-famed tree, man;
And blythe we'll sing, and hail the day
   That gave us LIBERTY, man. "

---

* This and other Odes by Burns expressing similar sentiments are still boycotted. W. Scott Douglas and A. Cunningham found fault with Robert Chambers for publishing such Odes. Robert Chambers himself says, that - *"Is there for honest poverty"* embodies "all the false philosophy of Burns' time, and of his own mind". These cringing editors have done much injustice to the "honest fame" of Burns. They should have seen themselves *as others see them*, in the Poet's letter of 13th April 1793, to Erskine of Mar, where he says - "I have often, in blasting anticipation, listened to some hackney scribbler, with the heavy malice of savage stupidity, exulting in his hireling paragraphs". These editors knew about the real date of *"Scots! wha hae"*, as far back as 1839.

And in the eighty-four preceding lines, the word "Britain" occurs twice, while, *as in Ogilvie's book*, Scotland is *conspicuous by its absence!* But this is not all, - precisely like Ogilvie, *he draws the line sharp and clear*, thus: -

" But seek the forest round and round,
And soon 'twill be agreed, man,
That sic a tree can not be found
'Twixt London and the Tweed, man ".

In the next verse a painful view of Scotland appears *between the lines:* -

" Without this tree, alake this life
Is but a vale o' woe, man;
A scene o' sorrow mixed wi' strife,
Nae real joys WE know, man.
WE labour soon, WE labour late,
To feed the titled knave, man;
And a' the comfort WE'RE to get
Is that ayont the grave, man. "

In the year 1795 the lessons of the French Revolution were beginning to make some headway in Scotland. An invasion was imminent. The NATION then evidently saw that although "*landed property cannot be removed*", the *removal* of the landlords presented very little difficulty. What a pity the "rabble" did not see eye to eye with the "NATION" at that time! The rabble were then invoked to defend their king and country. Mark the words *"their country"*. *Volunteer* (?) corps were formed in many districts in Scotland, Dumfries included. Burns *had* to join, and was forced to incur a deathbed debt in buying a uniform. In a ballad headed "The Dumfries Volunteers", composed in 1795, Scotland is again conspicuous by its absence: -

> " Oh, let us not like snarling curs
> In wrangling be divided,
> Till, slap, come in an unco loon,
> And wi' a rung decide it.
> Be Britain still to Britain true,
> Amang oursel's united;
> For never but by British hands
> Maun British wrangs be righted. "

These lines also form a key to "Scots! wha hae". Numerous keys can be had. Take, for instance, the following lines written by him in 1794 in a lady's pocketbook: -

> " Grant me, indulgent Heaven, that I may live
> To see the miscreants feel the pains they give:
> Deal Freedom's sacred treasures free as air,
> Till slave and despot be but things that were. "

These, it is obvious, were *living* miscreants, not the followers of "Proud Edward", and it is to them, *and them alone,* that he refers in September 1793, when he uses the words: -

> " Lay the proud usurpers low!
> Tyrants fall in every foe!
> Liberty's in every blow!
> Let us Do - or Die !!! "

Burns, like Ogilvie, was a philosophical admirer of English freedom as well as an ardent believer in the Revolution principles of 1688. He was not the man to revive Border feuds. The reference to Wallace and Bruce in "Scots! wha hae", doubtless was intended to rouse and stir up the "*rabble*" of 1793. The "woes and pains" and "servile chains" have nothing to do with England or "Proud Edward". Burns was thoroughly loyal to the *British Constitution:* at a volunteer festive gathering in 1795, when asked to give a toast, the following are the concluding lines of it: -

> " And here's the grand fabric, Our FREE
> CONSTITUTION,
> As built on the base of the GREAT REVOLUTION;
> And longer with politics not to be crammed,
> Be anarchy cursed, and be tyranny damned;
> *And who would to LIBERTY e'er prove disloyal,*
> *May his son be a hangman, and he his first trial !* "

These are brave words; and we can almost see not only the Dumfries *gentry* *, but also the Edinburgh *gentry*, "Old Braxy" included, cringing under the truth, justice, and heroism which inspired the soul of the author of "Scots! wha hae". In a country under tyrannical rule, as Scotland was then, it was only natural that about one half of the people should be Government spies and the other half cowards. Burns, although he was an excise-man at £50 a year, and only £35 when off duty on account of ill-health, was not a spy. Various attempts were made to coerce him to join the other *party*; and his *faith* was often put to the test in connection with "Loyal" toasts. On such occasions he took the opportunity of trampling on the maggots and flies which were then changing the British Constitution into a veritable mass of corruption. These parasites gloried in toasting *"King and Country!"* *Their* Country! and *their* King! Yet they expected the "rabble" not only to respond to such toasts, but, when any battles had to be fought *on behalf of the* "NATION", the "rabble" were expected to do this also.

---

* " There is reason to believe that, in his latter years, the Dumfries Aristocracy had partly withdrawn themselves from Burns, as from a tainted person. That painful class, stationed, in all provincial cities, behind the outmost breast-work of gentility, there to stand siege, and do battle against the intrusions of grocerdom and grazierdom, had actually seen dishonour in the society of Burns and branded him with their veto, had, as we vulgarly say, *cut* him! Alas! when we think that Burns now sleeps 'where bitter indignation can no longer lacerate his heart', and that those fair dames and frizzled gentlemen already lie at his side, - where the breast-work of gentility is quite thrown down, - who would not sigh over the thin delusions and foolish toys that divide heart from heart, and make man unmerciful to his brother! "
- Thomas Carlyle, 1828.

Nay, the "rabble" were, as a rule, coerced to fight the "NATION'S" battles. In the West Highlands, men were hunted, caught, and, if they refused to be sworn in, they were bound hand and foot, and thrown into a dungeon in the laird's house. They were dragged out of this dungeon once a day, and the soles of their feet, after being first rubbed with grease, were held up to a roasting fire. This repeated ordeal, as a rule, led to all the swearing-in required even in the making of a dragoon. In the Eastern Highlands (Aberdeenshire), "hanging by the heels" was sometimes resorted to as a preliminary to swearing-in.

Auld Willie MacPherson of Loch Kinnord, an octogenarian, who died a few years ago, used to tell of a widow's only son, who was murdered by the laird in that way. An eye-witness had described to him "what a terrible thing it was to see the poor fellow hanging by the feet, and the blood pouring out of his nose, eyes, and ears". This sight was, doubtless, *intended* to be a "terrible" one. Yes, to serfs and cowards. But to any human beings worthily called *men* or *women*, such a sight would be *revolting*, and we may assume that atrocious spectacles of that kind are possible only in countries where the inhabitants are brutalized by tyranny, and the human soul is steeped in the ignorance and superstition of priestcraft. We may safely conjecture that the parish clergyman dined with the laird the same day the murder was committed, and that he afterwards visited the sonless widow, and lectured her from *The Larger Catechism* "as to the great sin her foolish and wicked son had committed in rebelling against God's authority, of which the laird was only the instrument".

Burns and Ogilvie could not possibly be anything else than Revolutionists. They were not, however, tried before an Edinburgh jury; neither was Moses tried before an Egyptian Braxfield. Poor Thomas Muir did not grasp the nettle firmly enough. He was only a Reformer, and, being somewhat lamb-like in his ways, he was considered a tender morsel by the "hounds which growl in the Kennel of Justice", as Burns describes the Scotch Executive of *Law and Order* of his time.

Thomas Muir wanted to extend the franchise - to give people a *paper* vote - a phantom reform - which, compared with Ogilvie's scheme, may be described as a system of political tinkering, giving rise to disappointment on the one hand, and dis-satisfaction with increased discontentment on the other. Ogilvie's equal-share-in-the-land would carry with it, as the law of representation then stood, not only manhood suffrage, but womanhood suffrage also. And why not?

Ogilvie's single and simple remedy was quite ample for sweeping away the double and compound evils of modern landlordism, and we now see what a wise and practical radical reformer he was. But how sad to think, that we, in the British Isles, who boast so much of our civilization, are still kept in ignorance of those elementary truths regarding our natural rights. *Yes, kept!* It seems to be the special duty of those who "fatten on the wages of servility" to keep the people as ignorant as possible. And until recently any *"agitator"* who dared to instruct his fellow-men, in regard to their rights, was held guilty of high treason and sedition. This, by the way, is still a crime, not only in Ireland, but also in England and Scotland. Have we not lately witnessed the degradation of these so-called "free countries" by the arrest of Irish refugees on British soil. These things act as a spur to the slow but sure Revolution now going on in Ireland, and partly in Scotland; and no one can wisely grudge a *little spurring.* The BRITISH CONSTITUTION is no longer "the glory of Britons and the envy of foreign nations", as our parochial essayists used to tell us. Even England - "merry England" - the "home of freedom" - is not now so merry or so free as she once was; but it requires no prophet to foresee that her time of wakening up, and reverting to the Revolution principles of 1688 as a basis of restoring the Rights of her People, and the happiness of their homes, cannot be far distant.

Let us now look at the contents of a small but interesting manuscript - *interesting to the reader of* THE RIGHT OF PROPERTY IN LAND. It is unsigned, but it is undoubtedly in the handwriting of Professor Ogilvie: -

" PITTENSEAR, *September 12th 1776.*

" It seems highly probable that this distemper, what-ever be its nature, will remove me from the present scene.

" I ought surely to depart without reluctance and repining, having abundant reason to return thanks for that portion of life and that measure of good which I have already enjoyed, which seems to have exceeded, at least in tranquillity and contentment, the common standard of what is allowed to man. I have only to implore that some time may be allowed for the settlement of the affairs I leave behind me, and, if possible, to reduce into some form a synopsis at least of those contemplations and schemes which have occurred at various times to my mind, as of importance to the general welfare of mankind and the improvement of their present state.

" It ought to be my care to apply with assiduity whatever time is given to these respective purposes, but without anxiety or repining, because both these must necessarily be left very incomplete; to turn away my thoughts from all that is probable to take place in my affairs when I am here no more, except so far as may be useful in suggesting useful direction to my nearest friends to be left them in writing, but without subjection to any positive commands. May it please that Sovereign Power, from whom I have received so many good gifts, to grant me now ευθανασια [euthanasia] an easy and tranquil dismission from this mortal stage, or, if that may not be, at least may He vouchsafe that amid the pain and agonies through which I am to pass my patience may be sustained and the use of my reasoning powers remain undisturbed to the last parting pang. "

Pittensear, the reader already knows, was Professor Ogilvie's ancestral home. The date suggests many digressions which must be brushed aside. But one or two may be glanced at. The 4th of July 1776, had just given birth to the great American Republic, and the news of the event was creating some stir in the Mother Country. The domineering British landlords - the NATION ! - were busy *enlisting* the sons of the British "rabble" -

> " To cowe the rebel generation,
>   And save the *honour* o' the NATION ! "

The ignorant "rabble" *enlisted* and agreed to cut the throats of their cousins in America. It was *Law and Order*, and they were sworn by all that's holy to fight *for their King and Country!* But in reality they fought for the purpose of coercing the Americans to pay a tax upon tea, imposed by British landlords, to enable themselves to pocket more of the rents earned by the cultivators of British soil.

> " Safe in their barns, these Sabine tillers sent
>   Their brethren out to battle - why? - for rent:
> Year after year they voted cent. per cent.,
> Blood, sweat, and tear-wrung millions - why?
>   - for rent!
> They roar'd, they dined, they drank, they swore
>   they meant
> To die for England - why then live? - for rent ! " *

It is quite plain that the *Wealth of Nations* (published in 1776) did not come up to Ogilvie's expectations *in regard to property in land.* There is no doubt Adam Smith was boycotted by the *Law and Order* of those times, and coerced to modify and delete whole chapters referring to the landlords, as being seditious and unfit for publication. Ogilvie, as we have seen, had regard to a higher "power" than the *Law and Order* of a set of petty tyrants, when he formed his resolution to publish his

---

* **Byron - *"A Country Ruled by Rent"*. (Editor).**

"contemplations and schemes". His book is a monument of truth, wisdom, and courage. His magnanimity was unbounded; his heart overflowed with love and genuine sympathy towards mankind. Like Moses, he set himself to free an enslaved people: enslaved, because ignorant of their natural rights; powerless, because wanting the source of all power - knowledge. Like Moses, he advises mankind to take their stand, *upon the earth*, by practically adopting the *First Commandment* - Thou shalt have no other gods, dukes, earls, lords, landlords, or other land-grabbers, coming between you and the Creator of the earth, as regards the birthright of every human creature. He regarded not the alleged heavenly rights of earthly kings or their vassals. The golden calf of commercial landlordism he detested even more than all the superstitious kingcraft and priestcraft of ancient Egypt.

It is evident that *The Right of Property in Land* was the great aim of his life. Nay, more, we can see that it came forth from his soul as the fulfilment of a sacred undertaking with "that Sovereign Power, from whom", he acknowledges with overwhelming gratitude, he "received so many good gifts". He was then In his fortleth year. HIs health had utterly broken down through over-study and sedentary habits *. He

---

* **Letter from his friend and colleague, John Ross, Professor of Oriental Languages.**

recovered his health, and lived for upwards of forty-two years after this. He, however, did not allow much time to pass before he *reduced* "into form those contemplations and schemes which (had) occurred at various times to (his) mind as of importance to the general welfare of mankind and the improvement of their present state". The receipt for the cost of printing "*The Right of Property in Land* . . . and The Regulations by which it might be rendered more beneficial to the lower Ranks of Mankind", is dated 25th August 1781.

It is interesting to consider the manuscript of Ogilvie's *Essay* and the "synopsis" to which it undoubtedly refers. From the title page we can go to the *Introduction*, and there we find more of the *Pittensear schemes* "gradually unfolded". These schemes, it is of some importance to note, are the result of the author's *"own opinions, thinking freely and for himself"*. He tells us (in original unedited *Essay*) that "the leading principles of that system, which he now holds, respecting property in land have been *coeval in his mind with the free exercise of his thoughts in speculative inquiries*; they have recurred often, they have been gradually unfolded, and for some years past he has been accustomed to review them frequently, almost in their present form, with still increasing approbation".

Here we have a candid and straightforward author whose opinions, he himself tells us, are *new*. "All that he would request in their favour (and the candid will readily grant this) is, that they may not be rejected on a first disgust, and that those who cannot adopt the opinions here advanced *may at least bestow some pains in ascertaining their own!*"

There is a gentle touch of humane irony in these concluding words which is characteristic of the author. Other *gentle touches* will be met with throughout the work, but they are sometimes so very gentle that it is even possible to misapply them, as in the case of the words, "The poor you have always with you". For example, how seldom these words are interpreted thus: "The poor *you* have always with you . . .".

In the year 1786 Professor Ogilvie took the lead in an attempt to reform the system of education in the North of Scotland. Nothing could have surpassed in *perfection* the system of graduation which the Masters of King's College carried on in Ogilvie's time. Three days before the examination day, the questions, *and also the answers thereto*, were dictated by the masters to the students. This scientific mode of incubation, together with *the laying on of hands* and the incantation of the "graduation oath" could scarcely fail to bring forth a fully-fledged M.A. from almost every egg in the academic nest. The Professors had so little to do in those days that it was perhaps found expedient to have such a *gavelkind* system of distributing University honours as a sort of make-show. In the year 1770 the number of students in Marischal College was "near 120, and not above half that number at the King's". This was equal to an average of six pupils for each of the ten Masters of King's College, or, more correctly, eight or nine of a class for each teaching master, when we leave out the three *sinecurists* who were "never known to teach a class". (Excepting in one instance, where a Principal, who had been found guilty of having forged a Charter and an Act of Parliament, and of having committed "dilapidations," or "peculations " rather, of College revenues, was sentenced to lecture twice a week! *)

But Professor Ogilvie had other evils to put up with as a member of King's College. His colleagues not only alienated some of the lands belonging to the College, but they misapplied and "misappropriated" College funds. They also disposed of the patronage of no less than fifteen churches, and, worse still, the right of presentation to twenty bursaries. The great landlords were the purchasers of these saleable commodities, and in this way they became the

---

* **Evidence before Royal Commission of 1826.**

private owners of rights and duties which, until then, were held by the Professors in trust for the public. The money received for Church patronage has been accounted for, but the price of the other articles of commerce was appropriated by the Masters as their own private property. It became "money in their purse"!

It is superfluous to mention that Professor Ogilvie was not a silent witness or a consenting party to such proceedings. He was now in his fiftieth year, and finding that he had protested in vain as a member of Senatus for the long period of twenty-two years, he resolved to carry his appeal to the bar of public opinion.

A paper which was printed and circulated at this time, bearing the title "OUTLINES OF A PLAN *for Uniting the King's and Marischal Universities of Aberdeen, with a view to render the System of Education more complete"*, contains strong internal evidence that it came from Ogilvie's pen. It proposed various improvements, and, among others, that all sinecures should be abolished. The whole of the Professors of Marischal College were favourable to the scheme, but seven out of the ten Professors of King's College, the *"seven wise Masters"* as they were called, opposed it; and the reforms planned by Ogilvie in 1786 were not carried out until 1860.

Professor Ogilvie looked upon Universities as public institutions, and he considered that professors were merely public servants as regards teaching, and Trustees for the public as regards endowments, buildings, libraries, &c. The Masters of King's College who obstructed the proposed University reforms held very different views from Ogilvie. They not only scorned the idea of being considered public servants, but they unblushingly claimed the University and its endowments as their own private property. And why not? The seven obstructionists (of whom *only* three were sinecurists!) doubtless believed that their position, as a whole, was more justifiable than that of the landholders, who, as a rule, are *all* sinecurists, but whose "pensions and salaries" are by *law* established.

His letters concerning the affairs of the University furnish the only instance in Professor Ogilvie's life, where we find him revealing himself in his true character, as defender of the rights of the people; excepting another glimpse in 1764, when his name prominently appears in connection with a scheme for a *Public Library* in Aberdeen, which was to embrace the libraries of the Universities. With the exception of these two glimpses, Professor Ogilvie, as far as known, never disclosed his name to the public in connection with anything he did, or attempted to do, during the whole course of his long life. He loved tranquillity, and avoided publicity. It is not improbable that, after due deliberation, he came to the conclusion that his contemplations and schemes for the general welfare of mankind would have more effect if published anonymously than otherwise. His *Right of Property in Land* was read on the continent of Europe, as the work of an Englishman, who advocated the abolition of serfdom, and who was able to say: "Look at us *English*, how we have prospered since we became a free people, - you French, Germans, Poles, Russians, &c., want a revolution very badly, we had our last one in 1688; you are a full century behind us".

Professor Ogilvie must have rejoiced in the abolition of serfdom in France. The Revolution of 1789, ghastly in some respects, was only the natural outcome of what preceded it.

He also lived to rejoice in the still more sweeping land tenure reforms carried out in Prussia. "Nothing, probably", says Professor Fawcett, "has so powerfully contributed to promote the extraordinary progress of Prussia as the reforms which were carried out in her system of landed tenure, at the commencement of the present century, by Stein and Hardenberg. A feudal tenantry was transformed into cultivating proprietors, who have, probably more than any other class, contributed to the social and material advancement of Prussia." * These reforms were doubtless planned by Frederick the Great, and no reader of *The Right of Property in Land* would be surprised to learn that a copy of that work, marked "with the author's compliments", was found *inter alia* in the repositories of that famous monarch. Such a discovery would not be more surprising than that Professor Ogilvie had something to do with the land tenure reforms carried out by Lord Cornwallis in lower Bengal, in the year 1793.

Thomas Muir had a copy of *The Rights of Man* in his possession, and this was made the principal *crime* for which he was banished. Burns, in order to escape a similar fate, had to hide his copy, and *The Age of Reason*, with the blacksmith of Dumfries. Professor Ogilvie's works would be considered more criminal than these. The man who dared to deny the divine origin of rents and tithes, and, moreover, who boldly defined them as "the improvident regulations of *human* law", and who was able to cite Moses as his authority, would, doubtless, be considered more dangerous than the renowned Thomas Paine. It was, perhaps, on this account that no lair could be found in the Aberdeen University Library for a copy of *The Right of Property in Land*, while *The Rights of Man* did find a place in that consecrated ground. One of the books which Professor Ogilvie had beside him when

---

* *Manual of Political Economy*, London, 1874. p.201.

he died, was the University Library copy of *The Rights of Man;* and it is not improbable that the very last stroke of his pen was employed in reviewing that book, or in revising a new work on *The Rights of Man to the Land* - *how lost, and how to be regained.*

The schemes of Ogilvie, this "ingenious and accomplished recluse", pointed towards the possibility of *Paradise regained*, even on this earth. He had no grudge against the creator for having made the earth as it is - he declared against monopoly in land.   His "projects for the good of mankind" will stand the test of time.   When *Macaulay's New Zealander* visits England, it is not the ruins of her edifices that will engage his thoughts, but her neglected fields.   It is there he will read the story of her decline and fall. The game is the same everywhere.   A corrupt dog-in-the-manger governing class is formed, and idleness and taxes are enforced on a landless people, with the usual and consequent miseries, vices and crimes. This lesson is being learned even in America and Australia, with their men and women starving in the large cities, and compelled to

> ' beg a brother of the earth
> To give them leave to toil'.

The Land Question lessons in Joseph's life, and elsewhere occurring in Holy Writ, are systematically ignored and misrepresented by the majority of the clergy, bribed and corrupted by despots and politicians. A sermon, finding fault with Joseph, in regard to slavery, extortion, and evictions, or commending him for the comparatively moderate rents he fixed, would be apt, not only to displease The powers that be, but would be considered sedition and treason in some quarters. The clergy are, therefore, quite mum on the subject of all earthly things (tithes alone excepted), until there is some proposal to restore the land to the people, and then they out-lawyer the lawyers in maintaining what they call the "law of the land". They mean the law of the landlords. And they scruple not to hold up Moses (the Prince of Revolutionists) as a pattern of Law and Order! Even the Apostle Paul, who was treated as a rebel against Law and Order during the whole of his Christian life, is claimed as the principal godfather of "The Powers that be"! Paul had no faith in the Divine Right of tyrants, landlords, and magistrates.

In THE CONFESSION OF FAITH and CATECHISM, formulated by the English *Divines* of 1643, and adopted by the Scotch landlords in 1649 and 1690, as the "CONFESSION of the CHURCH of SCOTLAND", we can study the relation between the English divines (of Westminster) and the Scotch landlords.

It is significant to note that the latter, in Parliament assembled, on 5th February, 1649, proclaimed Charles II. King and Pope of Scotland; and, two days thereafter, they adopted this English *Confession and Catechism* - this weapon of extortion and eviction - this device by which the *Divine Right of Landlords* has been made an article of the *Christian Faith* in Scotland. The clergy got a little bribe at this time. The landlords gave up Church Patronage. But the Merry Monarch restored this *Divine Right* to the landlords after he was made King, Pope, and god of England. Again, and accompanied with the very same bribe *, the Scotch landlords, in 1690, re-adopted this *English Confession and Catechism*, as the "*Confession of the Church of Scotland*". The English had a Revolution in 1688, and one can easily see why the landlords of Scotland resorted to this ecclesiastical dodge of humbugging the people. The clergy were made to subscribe this Confession, and if they did not preach up to it, they perjured their souls. The Confession enjoined that the '*Powers* are ordained of God', and that the "virtues and graces" of Charles Ii., George IV., and the absentee landlords, described in *The Twa Dogs*, are to be imitated by the people! It is impossible to estimate the amount of evil wrought in Scotland by this document.

---

* In 1712, there was another shuttle-cock restoration of Church Patronage, after which the landlords held it until 1874, when the author of Coningsby allowed them £250,000, in name of "sacrilegious spoil", for once more relinquishing their "unhallowed booty"!

In 1844 Mr. Disraeli was evidently a formidable Land Leaguer, but, owing to the worship of landlordism by *all "sects"* of "religionists" at that time, he was powerless. Even a "respectable body of dissidents" like the newly-instituted democratic *Free Church of Scotland*, although the undoubted offspring of a revolt against a "factitious aristocracy", would not give him the least support. No wonder he, in 1849, when famine and eviction were doing their cruel work in Ireland and Scotland, "recognised in the Church the most powerful agent" of landlordism! The clergy then declared that famine and eviction were "visitations from God, sent as trials on the Faith of His own people"! The poor people - *poor devils* - "believed and trembled"! The *League* between religionists and landlords was a powerful one.

Many a kind-hearted and naturally noble-minded clergyman has fallen a victim to the ancient rules of his order. He is sworn to obey these rules in the same way as a judge is sworn to administer unjust laws. The root of the evil is landlordism. It is with its "spoil" that sovereigns, priests, judges, landlords, professors, policemen, soldiers, and other public servants are debased, corrupted, and bribed. "That exclusive right to the improvable value of the soil which a few men are permitted to engross", as defined by Professor Ogilvie (*Essay,* p.43), is "a most oppressive privilege, by the operation of which the happiness of mankind has been for ages more invaded and restrained, than by all the tyranny of kings, the imposture of priests, and the chicane of lawyers, taken together, though these are supposed to be the greatest evils that afflict the societies of humankind".

We pause at these words, and as they enter our souls we get a glimpse of the sage that penned them. We realise his animated presence within ourselves, in combination with the quickening truth presented to our understanding. Here we have the essence of Political Economy - the Land Gospel - compressed within the small compass of seventy-two words; and in one word - the word "permitted" - he has revealed to us both the diagnosis and the cure of the "greatest evils that afflict the societies of humankind". "A few men are *permitted* (by the many!) to engross a most oppressive privilege - *the exclusive right to the improvable value of the soil.*" This is the real cause why the happiness *of the many* has been invaded and restrained for ages! Kings, priests, and lawyers are merely scare-crows and puppets, and "a few men are *permitted*" to pull the strings! We have this fact on the undoubted authority of a man who was himself one of the "few", namely Professor Ogilvie.

In withdrawing the *permission*, which is the simple cure suggested, there is no word in his teaching about the question of compensation - not even as a temporary obstacle.   In the case, however, of *real* property, *created by labour*, he would fully compensate the real labourer for all loss sustained in connection with any of his benevolent schemes of land reform. The landholder has a right only to the "improved" - the created - value of the soil. He has no right to the "original and contingent value".   "That must still reside in the community at large, and, though seemingly neglected or relinquished, may be claimed at pleasure by the legislature, or by the magistrate, who is the public trustee."

The land belongs to "the community at large" ! We must not narrow the Land Question, as merely affecting the labourers or tenants of the soil, and their Lords and masters. Those who are not directly connected with these *Lords of Creation* are equally interested. The robbery which the landless labourers *permit*, in the shape of indirect taxation and expatriation, is more fraudulent, more pernicious, more cruel, more extensive and wide-spread than the robbery of rent. Land rent, however, we must not forget, is the root of all the robbery - the taxation of the landless people being merely the outcome. This is so very obvious, that I feel a kind of shame in mentioning it. Yet it is a fact we steadily ignore. We forget that the land belongs to the Nation - to the People - and that its rent is a national fund which should be used for national purposes - for the equal benefit of the whole People. We forget that the mere withdrawal of our permission of the abuse of National funds would leave us with a handsome surplus every year, after providing for free libraries, free schools, and free universities; and that all taxes and excise customs on industry or articles of consumption would cease to be necessary. We forget about the numbers of widows, orphans, aged or disabled workers, and other fit subjects of benevolence, who ought to be provided with pensions out of such a surplus, in a country which boasts of the Christian Faith. We forget the many lessons of the past, and we forget that we have permitted ourselves to get into this condition of forgetfulness, entirely through ignorance - positive ignorance - inculcated by the traditional tools of statecraft tyranny of the most pernicious kind ever known to exist, namely, landlordism.

Why is it that the laws of Moses have been disregarded as to *Property in Land?* Why is it that the gospel of Jesus has been topsy-turvied, perverted, and made subservient to landlordism and slavery? Why is it that such works as George Buchanan's *De Jure Regni,* John Locke's *Civil*

Government, Professor Ogilvie's *Right of Property in Land*, and Henry George's *Progress and Poverty* are not read in every cottage, and *authorised* to be taught in every school in the three kingdoms? And why is it that *"A man's a man for a' that"* is not sung as a sacred song, in every church, chapel, and Sunday-school, not only in the "Land of Burns", but in every land where the English language is spoken?

Submission to ignorance is a breach of Natural Law, and every breach of Natural Law is duly followed by its appropriate punishment. Such a transgression on the part of an individual, and most certainly on the part of a community, is followed by slavery, poverty, and misery. Kings, priests, judges, University professors, and even policemen, the moment they are permitted to forget their position as public servants, become tyrants and robbers, and prey upon society instead of guarding its liberty and property. They should be constantly reminded of their position and duties as trustees and servants.

Can the example of Moses help us here? Emphatically, Yes. He was not only the Prince of Revolutionists, but he was also the Prince of *Free Thinkers* and *Free Inquirers*. When "the angel of the LORD appeared unto him in a flame of fire out of the midst of a bush" (Ex. iii), what did Moses say?

- "And Moses said unto God, Behold, when I come unto the children of Israel, and shall say unto them, 'The God of your fathers hath sent me unto you'; and they shall say unto me, 'What is his name?' what shall I say unto them?" Moses was not to be satisfied with the *"God of his fathers"*, or the "God of Abraham"! he must have a God *for himself,* namely, the I AM. "And God said unto Moses, I AM *that* I AM: and He said, 'Thus shalt thou say unto the children of Israel, I AM *hath sent me unto you'.*" "And God said, moreover, unto Moses: 'This *is* my name for ever, and this *is* my memorial unto ALL GENERATIONS !' " It is not I WAS, or *my Fathers were,* but I AM !

Reader! have you got an I AM ? Because, if not, Nature has made a mistake; you should have been born with four feet, a long nose for smelling along the ground, and a tail which you could occasionally wag by way of expressing your reverence and homage for some *Master,* whose will, even when he is kicking you, *must be your pleasure!* Remember that every day brings forth its own light and heat, its own Truth and God, and the Truth and God of yesterday, like the light and heat of yesterday, are no longer available. The fossilised *"Jehovah"* of modern Theology is the God of the British House of Commons, and has been the God of that House for centuries, when making many anti-I AM laws: laws of oppression, coercion, slavery, wars, and murders, including the murders of starvation caused by the monopolising of land - preventing its use and cultivation. The landlords - murderers (!)? Yes. ST. GREGORY THE GREAT said so, more than twelve hundred years ago, long before Buchanan, the Saint-Andrews, Oxford, and Spanish Inquisition *"damnable heretic"*, was born: -

"Let them", said he, "know that the earth from which they are created is the common property of all men; and that, therefore, its products belong indiscriminately to all. Those who make private property of the gift of God pretend in vain to be innocent. For in thus retaining the subsistence of the poor they are the murderers of those who die every day for want of it."

Next to the I AM creed of Moses, who was the Greatest and Grandest of all *Spartans,* we have here, perhaps, the most clear and the most concise economic creed ever uttered or penned. But it is only an amplification of the I AM creed. The *First Commandment* is only an amplification of that same everlasting creed; and, as a *Declaration of Independence* - the independence of an enslaved people - the inspired and inspiring God-given words I AM are unsurpassably comprehensive, unsurpassably tyrant-proof, unsurpassably laconic.

From the *First Commandment*, the amplification proceeds in the *Second*, and enjoins the prevention of sham gods, sham dukes, sham lords, and "*dummies*" of all sorts; and implies the exclusion of all sham creeds descriptive of spurious gods recommended for "homage", "reverence", or "worship", in room of the I AM genuine God of mankind, the GOD of Liberty, Justice, and Impartiality.

From the *Second Commandment* the amplification still proceeds in the *Third;* and urges practical manliness on the part of mankind. "Thou shalt not take the name of THE LORD *thy God* in vain". You are not to palaver about this - any man who has the I AM spirit in him rebels at once against all forms of tyranny. There was much need of the *Third Commandment* in Scotland when Burns wrote his War Song -

    "Scots! wha hae wi' Wallace bled".

It is not to be wondered at that William Ogilvie took his *Political Economy* from the Books of Moses. He had the I AM spirit -

     "Let us Do - or Die!!!"

William Ogilvie and Robert Burns recognised only one divine Law and Order, only one Sovereign Power - that which governs the Universe, and guides the circling spheres. Examining the *Law and Order* of "divine" Kings, "divine" Ecclesiastics, "divine" Men of Rank, "divine" Olivers, and even "divine" Landlords *in Dei nomine*, what did they see? They saw a reign of usurpers, hypocrites, murderers, and robbers who had disfranchised the bulk of mankind, contrary to Natural Justice. The *Spectre of Democracy* was no terror to them. They assiduously prayed - *Thy Kingdom come: Thy Will be done* ON THIS LITTLE EARTH *as it is in Heaven.*

The fact of Professor Ogilvie, when verging on the allotted span of three score and ten, being still in the van of Land Law Reformers, agitating his benevolent schemes with "unabated fervour and vigour", amidst the storms and disasters of the French Revolution, and the despotic cyclone which was then raging, is a remarkable spectacle which even the eye of opposition cannot behold without a sense of admiration. Professor Ogilvie loved mankind and wished to see justice done all round; he *preached and practised* genuine christianity during the whole course of his life, and he continued faithful even unto death. How very different is the nominal Christian, who is goody-goody enough to admit the justice of abolishing slavery, oppression, and the legalised robbery of landlordism, but who, with a wise shake of the head, asks you, "What's the use of agitating, seeing that YOU and I will be dead long before any Parliament will pass a measure of that kind?"

Professor Ogilvie addressed himself in accordance with the Revolution principles of 1688, to "the sovereign, the legislature, or the real patriots of a country". He deplored that the British patriots of 1688, and the American patriots of 1776, failed in securing their "natural right of property in land" - to *"establish"*, he says, *"an arrangement of the highest importance to the general welfare of their fellow-citizens".* And he deplored that the French patriots of 1789 stopped short at peasant proprietorship - "whose labours", he says, "now (1805) seem to have subsided in the dregs of mere despotism". (See Ogilvie's unedited *Essay*).

But what did the British patriots get? Did they improve their position at Waterloo? For whom, and for what, did they shed their blood there? What was their quarrel with the French people, or even with Napoleon? These are awkward questions which the partial historian and other landlord menials do not care to answer. The reader will see most clearly how cruelly the peasants of the British Isles were be-fooled in those days, shedding their own blood and murdering Frenchmen for the sake of maintaining British Landlordism, with its wars, rack rents, oppressive taxes, compulsory idleness of the people, starvation, and crime; together with the debasing influence of a superstitious religion taught in every Parish, by which Jehovah, as "the God of Hosts," was directly blamed for all these evils, while the real evildoers were extolled as saviours of mankind; their very bloodhounds worshipped as gods, and graven images of them planted as idols throughout the land.

The Highlanders who responded to the trumpet of war in obedience to their chiefs, how were they treated after Waterloo? We know that on landing in England the remnants of the Highland Brigade were received in every town they marched through with perhaps as much real patriotic pride, honour, and kindness as ever fell to the lot of brave and victorious men; and as they proceeded Northwards to what, once upon a time, was *their own country*, the feelings of warm welcome seemed rather to increase than diminish, until, Alas! they came to one spot: -

" A dearer, sweeter spot than all the rest ".

"That", says *an applicant* under the *Scottish Crofters' Act* of 1886 - pointing to a glen - "is the place where my father was born and brought up. Like some other young men he was forced into the army, but it was on the express condition that his parents, and their posterity, should never be disturbed in the possession of their land. On his return home after the battle of Waterloo, instead of his home - the home of his ancestors - there was nothing but roofless walls, thresholds overgrown with grass, and the nettle and thistle in full possession, rooted round the old hearth stones. He, for a moment, distrusted his eyes. The unexpected sight of such desolation pierced his heart, and he felt stupefied. How cruel of the French bullets to have spared him for such refined landlord torture! It was a complete *Highland Clearance;* not a living soul was left in the glen to tell what had become of the people." This was the work of the Commercial Landlord   - the *Commercialised* Highland Chief, or, more properly, thief! the advocate of Freedom of Contract - freedom to do what he likes with the land, and to kick the people about, or away altogether, in accordance with his caprice, avarice, or pleasure. The same story, with sad variations, may be told of many a Highland glen. And, with equally sad variations, it could be extended to the Lowlands, to England, to Ireland, and, without any doubt, to British India. The British *nabobs* excelled all other freebooters, barring, perhaps, the Spanish Christians who plundered and murdered the natives of Mexico. The East India Company was a huge syndicate of *Commercial* landlords, the undoubted scum and dregs of British despotism; but, nevertheless, it was approved of and supported by the *"Christian"* Churches of Britain and their Missionaries under the pretext of carrying the Gospel to the downtrodden races of the East.

When the real duties of a Sovereign are systematically neglected, and when a "factitious Aristocracy" have entirely forgotten the rights of the people, by whose mandate alone they act as legislature, it is then high time that "the *real* patriots of any country" should waken up. The real *Trafalgar* when "England expects every *real patriot* to do his duty" has yet to be fought. The real invader, not the shadowy bogey of the French Revolution, has to be cut down by the axe of Justice, and all useless and noxious weeds which now cumber the land, have yet to be uprooted and cast away.

Ogilvie's distinguished pupil, Sir James Mackintosh, Recorder of Bombay, who vindicated the French Revolution, vindicated also, by anticipation, the Indian Revolution of 1858. But the mild and amiable Sir James, although a *vindicator* of Justice and Reform, was an exceedingly frail and timid *agitator*. He was somewhat like JEREMIAH, while his old *Master* Ogilvie was fashioned after the *ancient model* of MOSES.

To Professor Ogilvie's proposals of land law reform, Sir James furnished this *wet blanket* - "Practical effect here (in India) you must not hope!" He was only beginning to see that his old *master* really intended his *schemes*, not as mere "speculations," but rather to be adopted *practically*, "as of importance to the general welfare of mankind, and the improvement of their present state". In a letter to Professor Dugald Stewart of Edinburgh, dated "Bombay, November 2, 1805", the following reference occurs: "A nephew of Dr. Reid, a young gentleman of the name of Rose, has lately come out here as a cadet, recommended to me by a very ingenious and worthy person, though not without the peculiarities and visions of a recluse, Mr. Ogilvie of King's College, Aberdeen." We have already seen how imperfectly informed Sir James must have been, in regard to "this most ingenious and accomplished recluse". He seemingly had no idea that Professor Ogilvie was possessed of more practical knowledge of agriculture, and the true relation of landlord and people to the land than perhaps was possessed, in the aggregate, by all the political philosophers of his time, the celebrated Adam Smith being thrown in along with the rest. He was by far too honest a man to attempt to write on any subject until he had first mastered the facts. The *Essay* itself is the best proof of this, and it would be impertinent to assert that the author was a practical and scientific man unless his work could stand the test of cross-examination. But nevertheless, the notion that he was only a *visionary and speculative recluse* was prevalent. That was one way of opposing his admittedly just and benevolent schemes. "What is the use", some would say, "of any schemes, however good, however benevolent, if they are not practicable *in this world? The next* is the place for these things! Therefore, any advocate for happiness *in this world* must be treated as a very dangerous heretic." We may guess the reason why Professor Ogilvie was a "recluse!"

The author of Birthright in Land was a thoroughly practical man. We have already seen that he was a born landlord: that he inherited the lands of Pittensear. His father, and also his grandfather, did not belong to the idle landlord, good-for-nothing gentry; they were intelligent farmers, and keen improvers of land, who cultivated one-third of the property as a manor farm, the remaining being let to tenants; and he continued in the footsteps of his sires as Laird of Pittensear up to the year 1772. He then sold the property to the Earl of Fife, but reserved to himself for life a lease of the mansion house and manor farm, which he retained "to the last parting pang". Ogilvie's father's Will burdened the family property to the extent of 4500 merks in favour of his sisters, and very probably this led to the sale. We gather that he had early experience as a landlord, as a gentleman farmer, and subsequently, from 1772 to 1819, as a tenant farmer, paying rent to the Earl of Fife.

In the year 1773 our "Agitator" and ex-landlord purchased for £1500 the property of Oldfold and Stonegavel, situated on Deeside, about six miles from Aberdeen. He held it for thirty-five years, and when he sold it, in 1808, the price he received was £4000. But the difference was not all profit. About the year 1798 he borrowed £2000 from his old friend, the Duke of Gordon, and of this sum he expended £1910 in draining, trenching, and blasting, and more than the balance was paid away in connection with the valuation and purchase of tithes.

In the year 1802 we find him carrying through a Process in the Court of Teinds, by which he saved the property from being plundered by increased tithes on the increased value arising from his improvements. He got the tithes valued according to the old rental. The tithes or teinds were then fixed at £9 10s., of which only £1 8s. 8d. reached the Parish Minister, the balance going to the tithe-owner, which happened in this case to be the Crown. He knew how to prevent the tithe-owner, and also the parson, from robbing the labourer of the value of his improvements on the land, and he adopted the proper precaution. The Process he raised, besides fixing the value of the tithes, concluded for a sale of the surplus to himself, and decree was obtained accordingly, for the sum of £68 5s., being at the rate of nine years' purchase of the amount of surplus or "free teind".

We see that "our accomplished recluse" was not a mere theorist who allowed his mind to run after what is called utopian fancies. The practical knowledge displayed in the *Essay* he manifested in a material manner on the barren lands of Oldfold and Stonegavel. "There is", says he, "no natural obstacle to prevent the most barren ground from being brought by culture to the same degree of fertility with the kitchen garden of a villa or the suburbs of a great town". And he tells us how to do it. But those readers who are not acquainted with the principles of agriculture, and who also are strangers to the principles of morality and justice, cannot be expected to appreciate the author's knowledge, unless we drag them to the very ground upon which he carried out his experiments, and there show to them the fruit of his labours, in the shape of an extraordinary increase in what we shall call *earned* increment.

The property of Oldfold and Stonegavel changed hands about thirteen years ago, when the trustees of a Widows' Fund in Aberdeen purchased it at £12,000, as an agricultural subject, and merely as an investment, without any mansion-house, or woods, or any value for sport. Prior to 1757 it only yielded a yearly rent of about £12, being then in its natural state, and let to a sheep farmer. The yearly rent it yields now is about £410, and the gross annual value produced, let us estimate at, say, £1640, when we take landlords (freeholder and feuholder), farmers, labourers, tradesmen, and merchants, &c., who all get a share, into account. Its gross annual value, produced from a stock of sheep and the labour of one miserable herdboy, up to the year 1757, would not exceed £36.

It will be seen that the rise in the producing value of this property is much greater than the rise which has taken place in its selling price. The rise in the price, let us observe, was a direct benefit to the owners, while the rise in its producing value benefited the whole community; a fact, by the way, which the advocates of absolute private property in land should note, in regard to their dog-in-the-manger doctrines about waste land, game preserves, and pastures, while there is one idle Briton who is *willing* to work, and who wants land for cultivation and improvement.

The facts and figures connected with Oldfold and Stonegavel embrace an object lesson, apart from their interest in giving us a glimpse of the author of *Birthright in Land*, successfully putting in practice the principles laid down in his *Essay*.

The truth as seen and presented to us by William Ogilvie, is a truth which is apparent to all, if people would only make use of their eyes. The main object of his Essay was to make the light of Truth shine into the souls of mankind, whose passive obedience to injustice and tyranny is entirely due to "the established rules of which are in every country accounted permanent and immutable, as being fixed by the destination of Nature" - of God. The "cultivators have no clear perception of the injustice and oppression which they suffer. They feel indeed, and they complain, but do not understand, or dare not consider steadily, from what cause their grievances take their rise" (*Essay*, p.51). And there be some tyrants who cannot help believing that they are doing God's work, because they are brought up in a faith which teaches that to rebel against them is the same as to rebel against Him. Trade unionists and blacklegs war against each other, and both parties are equally ignorant of the real cause why one man has to beg of another "for leave to toil"! and they blindly *tramp* the remedy under their feet.

What has become of every Briton's birthright share in the Country - in the Land? It is a huge fraud, and the most impudent, the most criminal, as well as the most extensive, ever committed since the creation. Think of it for a moment. The landlords abolished military tenure, and substituted money payments for military services. Then they pocketed this money for their own private use, and raised other money by taxes on the landless people, and by loans, *to pay for military expenses.* The most of the military money, by the way, was paid to themselves, their sons, and sons-in-law, in the shape of *military pay* and *pensions.* No wonder Lord Byron exclaimed: "War was rent!" Yes! they not only raised the price of the fruits of the earth, and thereby raised rents, which they, by a show of law, pocketed, but they also pocketed the bulk of the war taxes and war loans, and, on this account, they schemed and carried on war as a most profitable business: -

" Farmers of War! dictators of the farm;
  Their ploughshare was the sword in hireling hands,
  Their fields manured by gore of other lands. "

Surely the united common-sense of England, Scotland, brave little Wales, and Ireland, will bring about a day of reckoning! Surely that day is not far off when the Domesday Book will be looked into, and the titles to all the land in these Isles will be examined.

The Lords of the soil, let us repeat with emphasis, abolished the *only* title, the *only* tenure, the *only* alleged right *they* had to the soil - they abolished *military tenure*. They did so in England in 1672, and in Scotland in 1747; and they have had no tenure of any kind ever since, barring the self-established tenure of Freebooting.

"How preposterous, says Professor Ogilvie, "is the system of that country which maintains a civil and military establishment by taxes of large amount without the assistance of any land-tax at all ! In that example may be perceived the true spirit of legislation as exercised by landholders alone" (*Essay*, p.41). See also p.48, where he says: "that their large incomes (from land rents) are indeed pensions and salaries of sinecure offices!" He was an eye-witness to the robbery which was perpetrated in Scotland in 1747, when military tenure was abolished, and the land, with all its rents and royalties, finally taken from the people by the darling Whigs, the Tories agreeing, the Courts of Law agreeing; and, let us note, that the "Protestant" Clergy have not to this day made any *protest* against that robbery.

The history of Scotland, if written with the pen of truth, might be made most instructive to the whole human race. How did Scotland stand in Professor Ogilvie's time? The sleight of hand - to borrow that view of it from the language of Lord Salisbury - by which military tenure and "clannish tenure" were "slipped" into the present tenure of *commercial landlordism*, "entirely to the advantage of the landlords", meant the people were indiscriminately robbed. The rank and file who fought *for George* (!) at Culloden were robbed as well as the so-called rebels of those days. Where was the *Law of the land* then?

Let us here *note* that every man, woman, and child killed by the *Royal Army* after the battle of Culloden was a clear case of murder. Every tenant was bound by the *Law of the land*, until 1747, *to follow his feudal chief to the field.* And the so-called *rebels* who followed their *feudal lords* under the banner of Prince Charlie in the '45, did so in accordance with the *Law and Order* then in force. Had they refused, they would then have been *real* rebels. Consequently, we find that not a single individual *of the rank and file* of the "rebel" army could be tried in a Court of Law, hence the necessity of shooting and hanging them without the ceremony of a trial. The Duke of Cumberland, upon the whole, seeing that he was only a mercenary soldier, who took his orders from the Duke of Argyll, the real ruler of Scotland at the time, did his part of the work with as much humanity as could be expected of a professional master "butcher" of human beings. We have this on the authority of the Scottish, and also of the English Protestant clergy, in the praises and prayers they sent up (!) in favour of his good deeds.

The indiscriminate plundering, as well as murdering, which went on after Culloden, produced many songs and ballads in favour of "Bonie Prince Charlie". The idea of personal liberty or justice - except through some "anointed" despot - did not then exist. But there was, at least, one noble exception, The Rev. John Skinner, who in the last verse of his "Song of songs" - *Tullochgorum*, cursed the *fig-tree* Christians of his time in the following manner: -

" But for the sullen, frumpish fool,
   That loves to be Oppression's tool,
   May envy gnaw his rotten soul,
      And discontent devour him;
   May dool and sorrow be his chance,
      Dool and sorrow, dool and sorrow,
      Dool and sorrow be his chance,
         And nane say, 'Wae's me for him!' "

The clergy after the '45 did their utmost to extinguish the *soul of freedom* in Scotland, while they themselves, especially the State clergy, held a high old time of it, domineering over the people and wallowing in whisky punch. If anyone mentioned injustice, oppression, or tyranny, he was instantly gagged.

Military tenure, we have seen, was abolished in 1747. As a youth Ogilvie witnessed that *juncture* - that *favourable opportunity* - whereby the Scots might have got their natural rights restored "had they been themselves aware of their title to such rights" (*Essay*, p.63). A large portion of Scotland was then "nationalised": the estates of the rebel chiefs were forfeited to the Crown. But how much of these lands was given to the people? Not one square inch was given even to the *"loyal* men" who fought and conquered the "rebel" army at Culloden!

The same Act of Parliament which abolished military tenure abolished also the feudal hereditary jurisdiction of all the landlords in Scotland. Until then we must not forget that the landlords had the power to hang, drown, or dungeon the people as they liked, just as they now have the power to shoot grouse, deer, and other wild animals; but with this difference, that there was no close time - they could hang people all the year round! It was a great privilege, and one upon which the majority of the landlords put some value; and, of course, they lodged a claim for compensation!! The matter was decided in the Court of Session in the year 1748.

They claimed the sum of £1,587,090 sterling, and that Court allowed £152,037 12s. 2d. as a redemption price of the sole right and privilege of that form of Scottish landlord sport in all time to come.

Let the reader imagine that all the excisemen in the British Isles somehow got all political power into their own hands, that they then demitted their offices and put in a claim for compensation for giving up the pleasure connected with smuggler-hunting, including occasional bribes for *letting people off*. (The landlords took *fines*, which is only another word for *bribes*.) These retired excisemen then vote public money to pay this "compensation", a puppet King gives the necessary assent, the Bishops in the House of Lords say *Amen!* and all curates and clergy throughout the country echo *Amen!*

Then these excise *lords*, let us say, keep all the excise duties to themselves; they manage all the distilleries and breweries as their own private property; they raise the excise duties to any rate they like: being proprietors *by law established*, who can interfere with them "to do as they like with their own"? They *"impose"* duties on other things; they tax everything under the Sun except distilleries and breweries; they tax the Sun itself for several years (the window tax); and they make the people pay the salaries of the new excisemen, who, by the way, are kept as mere flunkies to these idle lords. This imaginary swindle is only like a drop in the bucket as compared with the appropriation by the landlords of all the land - all the productive powers of Nature, necessary for the sustenance and enjoyment of the community - *Community!* Verily the bigger swindle has actually been perpetrated, and we still assert that *the age of miracles and witchcraft has gone by.* What meaning has the word "community" now?

The Rev. John Skinner was a sturdy Land Leaguer in his day, who used his pen in prose as well as in verse in favour of the people's cause. And it is not improbable that he and Professor Ogilvie *compared notes* on the Land Question as well as other things. But like the *Twa Dogs,* this must be left to the reader's own conjecture, for want of direct evidence. It is, however, worth noting that these three Land Leaguers, *Tullochgorum, Luath,* and Ogilvie, *alias Caesar,* were all closely connected, *and associated,* under the genial patronage of one man, namely, Alexander, fourth Duke of Gordon. It is also worth noting, as a special feather in Professor Ogilvie's cap as his tutor, that this nobleman was a model landlord, whose example and influence in the North of Scotland in those dark days cannot be overestimated. Notwithstanding this, the memory of Duke Alexander, *"The Cock of the North",* and the author of the most popular version of the song *"The Reel of Bogie"*, has been buried in oblivion almost as completely as the memory of his accomplished tutor.

Thanks, however, to Burns for his picture of *Bonie Castle Gordon.* We there get a view of the "princely" manner in which Professor Ogilvie's pupil performed his duty and office of landholder. He was not a sinecurist, neither did he belong to the *commercial* or *"guinea's stamp"* tribe of landlord. Burns visited Gordon Castle on September 7, 1787, and made the following *note* in his Diary: "Fine palace, worthy of the noble, the polite, the generous proprietor: The Duke makes me happier than ever great man did - noble, princely; yet mild, condescending and affable, gay, and kind - the Duchess charming, witty, and sensible - God bless them!" These everlasting words have embalmed the memory of one of "the worthy and humane *English* landholders", who resided in the so-called *"Northern Counties of England"*, to whom Professor Ogilvie dedicated his *Essay.*

Burns draws a comparison between the management of India's plains, under *The Company,* and of the *Bonie Castle Gordon* domains, under the pupil of Professor Ogilvie. The reader already knows that Professor Ogilvie took a keen interest

in Indian land-law reform. Did he meet Burns at
Bonie Castle Gordon, and did *they twa* then
discuss about Indian landlordism? If they did not,
it then becomes even more interesting to trace the
strong affinity which existed between the
contemporary souls of these two remarkable men.
But regarding probabilities, it is right to add that
one of Professor Ogilvie's sisters was married to
William Tod, the Duke's Factor at *Bonie Castle
Gordon,* and that the Professor was a frequent
visitor there. Dr. Currie might have assisted us here,
but we know why in those days he had to hide
the date of

" Scots! wha hae wi' Wallace bled ".

Perhaps for a similar reason he kept his
thumb on the name of that *anonymous* "gentleman"
he describes as "a particular acquaintance of the
Duke", who delivered the Duke's invitation to the
Poet's fellow-traveller "in all the forms of politeness",
in order to prolong the Poet's visit at *Bonie
Castle Gordon.* In the case of hidden facts -
purposely and systematically hidden - the inquiring
mind naturally, and by the law of necessity, takes
refuge in its own conjecture. In those dark days, in
the "Northern Counties of England", several other
"princely" landholders, besides the Professor's own
special pupil, rowed in the same boat with Ogilvie.

The *poor* Scot in those days had to cringe under tyranny, with an alternate choice of starvation at home or slave-driving abroad. We know that even Burns was only prevented from becoming a slave-driver by "the accidental delay of the vessel in which he had taken out his passage for Jamaica", and the almost equally accidental friendly intervention of The Rev. Dr. Blacklock. "I had", says the Poet in his letter to Dr. Moore, "composed the last song I should ever measure in Caledonia - 'The gloomy night is gath'ring fast', when a letter from Dr. Blacklock to a friend of mine * overthrew all my schemes, by opening up new prospects to my poetic ambition."

This was in the autumn of 1786. At this time, precisely, Professor Ogilvie was in the thick of his fight for Light and Truth in Aberdeen. The year 1786 marks a period of contemporaneous radical reforming eruption of the I AM spirit of these two men. It is perhaps not strange that their meetings, or correspondence, have been kept from the public eye to this hour, after all.

Has *British Christianity* in any way changed its creeds or tenets since those days of *"respectable professions"*? No! not one iota. Think about the idea

---

* **The Rev. George Lawrie of St. Margaret's Hill, Kilmarnock. Is it not remarkable that Providence made use of two *divines* to prevent Robert Burns from leaving Scotland in those days? Scotland should not forget these two men. They should be entered as *St. Thomas* and *St. George* on the roll of Scottish Saints.**

of Jesus Christ being in the flesh in Britain at the present time, and holding His tongue about the doings of landlordism - think of Him on a platform, supporting His Grace the Duke of Argyll ! Think of Him sneering at the numerous atrocities in Ireland, for which Lord Salisbury has made Her Majesty directly responsible! - Her Majesty, who is the Head, as Vicar of Christ, of the Christian Churches of England and Scotland ! We must swallow all these and many other things about Jesus, along with landlordism and other forms of robbery, in order to be within the fold of orthodox British Christianity!

The Duke of Fife (who bought Pittensear from Ogilvie) is, comparatively speaking, an honest commercial landlord, his ancestors having acquired the land as land merchants. 'Tis different with all the old feudal Dukes, Earls, and Lords, because the only title deeds they can show to their lands constitute complete evidence that their ancestors stole these lands.

Nevertheless, the Duke of Fife does not feel free from risk. He is, therefore, selling his lands in Scotland as fast as he can. He knows that his title deeds are worse than useless. They prove that he is in possession of stolen property - the property of the People! They prove that all his lands are liable for the *National Debt!* They prove that the People, or, to put it technically in order to drive the fact into the thick skulls of ignorant lawyers, *that the Crown, the feudal Superior of all landlords, as Trustee for the People*, can legally and justly impose the SINGLE TAX, *and tax all lands to their full value.* And it is no answer to the People's claim that a landlord, or his ancestors purchased the land; otherwise the Duke of Argyll and a few other dukes and lords might at any time sell England, Wales, Scotland and Ireland to Mr. Winans, or to the Emperor of Russia.

The following paragraph is taken, word for word, from a boycotted book, written by Sir George MacKenzie of Rosehaugh, and published by *Royal Authority* in the year 1678, bearing the title: "The Laws and Customes of Scotland in matters Criminal". Sir George is referred to as a believer in the *divine right of Kings,* but it is quite clear that he did not believe in the *divine right* of "Oppressors, thieves, *and other great men!"* This passage, be it observed, is taken from his Chapter on ROBBERY: -

"The Crimes answering in the Civil Law to oppression were *vis publica, vis privata,* and *concussio.* Those were punishable, *l. julia de vi publica,* who raised arms, or did violently eject men out of their houses or lands; those who assisted the

Oppressors with men are guilty thereof, and the punishment was *aquae et ignis interdictio . . .*". *

Sir George is almost the only Scottish Lawyer ever known to have done anything for Liberty and Property, hence the reason he and his books have been systematically boycotted to this hour. When the judges of the Court of Session banished all the members of the Scottish Bar from Edinburgh, in obedience to a letter from Charles II., George Mackenzie appeared before them as "a gentleman", he said, and he made these obsequious functionaries and also their royal master sprawl under his feet. He, notwithstanding his weakness for the divine right of kings, on that occasion manfully vindicated the divine right of every man to defend himself, and to oppose tyranny, injustice, or impudence in a king as in a beggar.

No country in the world can boast of better laws than Scotland. It is, however, not necessary to reiterate how these laws were broken, and by whom; or to make any comment regarding the punishment which might and ought to be inflicted on the breakers of these laws.

---

* **State and individual violence, and assault and battery, punishable, by Roman Statute, by immersion in water and burning or branding (*interdictio* is likely a misprint of *iuris dictio* - "judgement"). (Editor).**

There is more than one reason for giving a place in these *Notes* to a letter, written to GENERAL WASHINGTON by the Earl of Buchan, the mutual friend of Burns and Ogilvie: -

" DRYBURGH ABBEY, *28th June, 1791.*

" SIR, - I had the honor to receive your Excellency's letter. . . . May that Almighty Being, who rules over the universe, who presides in the councils of nations, and whose providential aid can supply every human defect, consecrate to the liberties and happiness of the American people a Government instituted by themselves for public and private security, upon the basis of law and equal administration of justice, preserving to every individual as much civil and political freedom as is consistent with the safety of the nation. . . . I have entrusted this sheet, inclosed in a box made of the oak that sheltered our great Sir William Wallace after the battle of Falkirk, to Mr. Robertson of Aberdeen, a painter, with the hope of his having the honor of delivering it into your hands. . . . I beg leave to recommend him to your countenance *as he has been mentioned to me favourably by my worthy friend Professor Ogilvie of King's College, Aberdeen.* . . .

" I am, with the highest esteem, Sir,
" Your Excellency's most obedient and
" obliged humble servant,
" BUCHAN. "

It would seem from the words now italicised that Ogilvie and Washington were not unknown to each other; and it is highly probable that the latter was presented with an early copy of *The Right of Property in Land*, and with some manuscript notes besides. He refers to *North America* (in his original unedited *Essay*) as having "lately enjoyed an opportunity of new modelling the establishment of landed property, even to theoretical perfection".

If Professor Ogilvie visited Dryburgh Abbey in June, 1791, he would then be within a day's ride of the abode of Burns. Trying to catch the *Twa Dogs* together, oddly enough we again come upon a suppression of dates and names.

"*In the summer of* 1791", says Dr. Currie, "two English gentlemen, who had before met with Burns in Edinburgh, paid a visit to him in Ellisland. He received them with great cordiality, and asked them to share his humble dinner - an invitation which they accepted." They did not leave before midnight - they "forgot the flight of time and the dictates of prudence". No wonder; for Burns, as described *by one of the party* to Dr. Currie, "was in his happiest mood, and the charms of his conversation were altogether fascinating. He ranged over a great variety of topics, illuminating whatever he touched. He related the tales of his infancy and of his youth; he recited some of the gayest and some of the tenderest of his poems: in the wildest of his strains of mirth he threw in some touches of melancholy, and spread around him the electric emotions of his powerful mind."

Who were these two *"English* gentlemen", and in particular what name shall we call the one who gave the information to Dr. Currie; and why should Dr. Currie suppress the name of any real Englishman? One thing is clear - *Twa* sympathetic souls - whether they were *the* "Twa Dogs" or not - did meet and spend a happy night together.

Considering the state of poor Scotland then, and the watching by spies of all the movements and meetings of persons suspected of being possessed of any genuine I AM spirit, Professor Ogilvie, no doubt, found it necessary as a rule to travel *incognito in his own country* - most likely as an *Englishman*, keeping his thumb upon the meaning of his own phrase - *"the Northern Counties of England"*. He wrote his *Essay* as an *Englishman*, and inscribed it to *Englishmen* !

We can hardly realise now-a-days the dangers and difficulties that a reformer like Professor Ogilvie had to contend with in his time - a time when the Soul of Freedom had, in truth, fled from Scotland. There is no doubt whatever of this, that if his notions of land-law reform had been fully known to the landed *gentry* and clergy, his life would have been taken either by a paid assassin, or by a stirred-up mob. He was an "ingenious recluse", and thus escaped more successfully than his renowned contemporary Dr. Priestley *, whose house was burnt and his books and manuscripts torn and strewed for miles along the public road, while he himself had to run for his life. This was the work of a befooled English mob, led by - we know - and marching to the old familiar tune of "The Church in danger". But in Scotland similar outrages were perpetrated in those days by *Law and Order!*

A military rabble, led by "epauletted puppies", to use the designation handed down to us by Burns, sacked the house of the Rev. John Skinner, carrying with them his books, manuscripts, and "everything". They spared his Manse, but they burnt his Church to the ground. More than once *Tullochgorum* saved his life by "skulking" in some hiding place, or "attiring himself in the garb of a miller, to escape the observation" of the military miscreants of those times.

---

* The Rev. Robert Hall of Cambridge, who defended Dr. Priestley and vindicated the French Revolution as well as British Liberty, was an ardent disciple of Professor Ogilvie. He attended his lectures during four sessions (1781-85), and was charmed with his translations of the Roman poets, which, in a letter to a friend, he described as "extremely elegant". It is well known that Robert Hall and Sir James Mackintosh were fellow-students, but few are aware that they studied under such a teacher as the author of *Birthright in Land*.

We can imagine the pangs felt by the highly sympathetic soul of William Ogilvie for the "woes and pains" of others, in those days. As regards his own personal sufferings, his *weep-not-for-me* spirit almost arrests us from referring to them in these pages. In his soliloquy of 1776 we see a man who could bravely and contentedly face death itself, "without reluctance and repining". "Having", says he, "abundant reason to return thanks for that measure of good which I have already enjoyed, which seems to have exceeded, at least in tranquillity and contentment, the common standard of what is allowed to man".

We, however, cannot skip over another "rude" and equally "unseasonable visit", as a companion picture of the period. When the so-called *Royal Army* was passing through Morayshire in 1746, a short halt was made at Pittensear House, and three cannon shots were fired at it. One of these shots struck the front wall close to the dining-room window, and, we need not say, caused the inmates much alarm. William Ogilvie, then about ten years of age, in all probability witnessed that scene - a sad example of what even a *Whig* Government may do at the head of a mercenary army. He, without any doubt, surveyed the wreck after the storm had passed. We have it on the authority of old people still living near Pittensear, that his mother, who happened to be in childbed at the time, never recovered the shock of that day's proceedings, and that shortly thereafter she was laid in a premature grave. And a few years later, when his disconsolate and broken-hearted father had quitted life's stage, he was left alone, in place of both father and mother, as guardian to four orphan girls. Here we may trace the way in which, what we may call a *motherly feeling* towards all the children of men, was developed in his breast. His *Essay on the Right of Property in Land,* in every line of it, says: *Suffer little children to come unto me,* and I shall teach them that *God is no respecter of persons;* that all *the children of men* are entitled indiscriminately to an equal share in the soil, in all wild animals, game, fish, and the whole products of nature, necessary for man's subsistence or enjoyment; and that anything contrary to this doctrine is a gross and blasphemous slander on the Creator, as well as a most iniquitous fraud on the bulk of mankind.

> Vive, vale. Si quid novisti rectius istis,
> Candidus imperti; si non, his utere mecum.

> " So goodbye and take care.
> And if you can propose anything
> more just than what's said here,
>   tell me frankly what it is.
> But if you can't,
> See you make good use of this
>   just as I do. " *

---

* **Editor's translation.**

Appendix to the Notes

" Resolutions by the Skye Crofters, passed at Meetings addressed by
MR. HENRY GEORGE
in January, 1885. "

The following benevolent principles of *Land Reform*, so much on Professor Ogilvie's lines, were adopted in Skye, as preached by Mr. Henry George, before the *Essay* now re-published was unearthed: -

" Whereas the land was made by God, who is no respecter of persons, for the equal use and enjoyment of all the people whom He brings into life upon it, we hereby declare, that any system which compels the people to pay rent to other human creatures, for the privilege of living upon God's earth, is a robbery of labour, and a wicked violation of the benevolent intention of the Creator.

" *Resolved.* - That while we shall thankfully welcome any measures that will lessen the tyrannous power which the so called landlords of Skye have exercised over us, we will not consider any measure as a settlement of the land question which does not restore our God-given rights in our native soil, *and does not restore the same full rights to our brethren of the cities, towns, and mineral and agricultural districts of England, Scotland, Ireland, and Wales,* by taking all rent for land for the common benefit of the whole people, and putting an end to the wicked wrong which compels labouring men to want, suffering, and untimely death, in order that idlers may live in luxury.

" *Resolved.* - That we call upon our brethren, *the working men of the whole country,* to give us their support in obtaining our natural rights, as we shall give them ours in obtaining theirs, and especially we call upon them to enter their strongest protest against the invasion of Skye by armed forces from the mainland, with the object of enabling the landlords to deprive us of the means necessary for the support of our families, by virtue of laws in the making of which we have had no voice.

" *Resolved.* - That the attention of the Right Hon. Sir Wm. Vernon Harcourt is hereby called to the unconstitutional manner in which the Sheriff and Procurator-Fiscal of the County of Inverness have acted with regard to the people of Skye, and that he is hereby requested to institute an open inquiry into their proceedings, with a view to their impeachment, removal, and punishment, and that the present

Commissioners of Police of the County be at once suspended, and a measure introduced into the next session of Parliament abolishing all such hereditary-landlord-authorities * not founded on the voice of the people.

" *Resolved.* - That this meeting tender heartfelt thanks to the Right Hon. W. E. Gladstone for having successfully carried through Parliament an Act which enables crofters, for the first time, to exercise their right in the making of laws which affect their interests. "

It is from little insignificant facts, observed here and there, that we are sometimes able to discover the course of human affairs, and those movements which now and again lead to the overthrow of long-established systems of despotism and slavery. We discover the currents of the sea by watching the ripples on the surface, and the mere *straws* which float in it.

---

* The *Local Government (Scotland) Act,* 1889, gave partial effect to this suggestion, but owing to the sickly condition of the children of Liberty in Lowland Caledonia, Scotland is still held under Landlord thraldom, excepting that the *Crofters' Act,* 1886, has produced an effect something like the taking of the *Bastille.* Rents in the Lowlands came tumbling down without any *Land Court!*

From on holiday in Strathpeffer, where
"the water is ferry goot, but ferry tangerous for all
teetotallers, or such as take too much of the dram,
and too much of the water itself is not ferry goot neither",
we hear -

The Rev. Maister Whatefer's

Chronicle of

Strathconon

- recorded by **DC MacDonald** -
edited from the 1891 Edition of *Birthright in Land*
by **Peter Gibb**

And as this antiquated Free Kirk "divine" humorously speaks
his mind, he seems to have some *agitating* surprises in store
even for himself. But, "*as for* myself" he asserts, "I am ferry
moderate in eferything - except *religion*" . . . .

" And it was these *pad*
landlords who refused to
kive a stance to puild a Free
Church   - themselves and the
Teffil together -   that kindled the
Highland Crofters to so much wicket
'agitation' in recent years, until, like
the   foolish   Galatians,   they   were
pewitched by ungodly Land Leaguers apout
more land, fair rents, and other worldly affairs,
instead of always minding the salvation of their souls.

And instead of attending prayer meetings and sermons - where the servants of the Lord had to preach in poats, and on the sea shore - they follow after false prophets like Henry George, going to Land League meetings, and packsliding ferry fast to the old wickedness of the pagpipes, and worldly songs of many ungodly poets like Purns, who was a ferry pad man when he was alive, and more so after he was tead. For his sinful song-book is still read out of sight in many places, which has a ferry 'unsettling tendency' for putting the poor against the gentry and the clergy, and making them forsake the *Confession of Faith* whatefer. The poor Free Church Ministers have had to keep up the panner of the Lord in the Highlands on ferry little pay, and ferry great hardships, since 1843.

"And, in some places, with ferry sore temptations; for, where the tyrants were like Pharaoh, it was ferry tifficult not to rise like Moses against them. Putt the gospel according to the Apostle Paul, as laid town in the *Confession of Faith*, must be obeyed whatefer. And people who came into this world to suffer, must suffer whatefer. And pad landlords, and unfair rents, and evictions, and even slafery, are all ferry useful, in their own way, for illustrating the doctrines of the Pible and for making the poor gif up all the joys of this world, and for putting their affections on things apove so as to withstand all sorts of trials on their faith.

"But Oich! Hoich! where will the Land Leaguers, and 'Agitators', and Purns, and Henry

George, and Parnell, and poor Gladstone if he toes not repent, go to? There will be plenty of primstone, and weeping and wailing, and knashing of teeth in that place whatefer, and they will get more than plenty of Home Rule from the Teffil, for all eternity, and for efer and efer Amen! For the Teffil was the first Home Ruler, and the first rebel, when he rebelled against God. And it is the Teffil that is now stirring up the people in Ireland and in the Highlands against the 'Powers that pe', which 'are ordained of God', as laid down ferry clearly in the Confession of Faith, which efery godly man is pound to sign.

"The Providence of God is ferry strange, for the rich are not always ferry happy in this world. King David and King Solomon were not ferry happy whatefer. And all this shows ferry clearly what pig fools the Crofters and the Irish are, when they pelieve what these ungodly Agitators tell them about fixity of tenure, fair rents, and free sale, for when kings and the gentry cannot he happy in this world with all their lands and money, how can the poor he happy, supposing they got all the land tivided among themselves tomorrow? And who is to rule over them, if the gentry was apolished? They would just pegin at once to kill each other as they tid in America apout slafery when they apolished it, which was also against the Confession of Faith whatefer.

"And there is no use saying more apout it whatefer, for there were always gentry and landlords and rulers and masters in this world, all by God's authority, and that must continue to pe to the end of time, for what *was*, must pe *is*, and the *is* of to-day will surely pecome the *was* of tomorrow, and so on, from *was* to *is*, and from *is* to *was*, to the last tay, when the Revelation of John comes to pass; and there shall pe no other future but *that* in this world whatefer. Putt there pe some infidels and radicals and other unpelievers, who tont pelieve in nothing - not even in the Teffil, or in Providence, not to speak of witches.

"There was only one agitator minister in the Isle of Skye, and *he was a pachelor;* and although he was a *Moderate*, the Free Church people got ferry fond of him, for he preached nothing but Land League toctrines in the pulpit, as well as at Land League meetings. And although he was very smartly tealt with, and also put in prison in Portree, still that pachelor minister went on, and tid a kreat teal of harm. He carried with him the agitation wherefer he went, and policemen and marines were sent to Tiree and Lewis, as well as to Skye, where the mischief at first pegan. And these marines tid no good against the agitation whatefer; but they encouraged it ferry much, and they were ferry friendly with the people, and they tanced and had singing concerts with the taughters of the crofters, and they proke the sabbath in many ways, which was a ferry bad example to the Highland people, and a tisgrace to Scotland as well. And it was not ferry goot *Law and Order* to preak the Law of God whatefer.

"These are only a few of the evils of the agitation, for I have said nothing apout the sufferings of Lord MacTonal in Skye, for want of his rents; or Lady Matheson in Lewis, for want of her rents; and many others, over and apove the Tuke of Argyll himself, who is a ferry godly man whatefer, for he is the President of the *Society for Propagating Christian Knowledge* in all Scotland, and the pooks that he circulates in the Highlands are not like Purns, or Shakespeare, or Carlyle, or Henry George, but they are all ferry safe pooks for the people to read. The Pible itself peing the only one which requires to be explained away in some tifficult passages py the ministers who are aple to do so: it peing impossible for priests and pachelor clergy to understand these passages whatefer. And a minister, with a wife and may pe twelve or more children, is always struggling like a poat in a storm, running for the shore. And when God sends help to him py the landlords, or other gentry, he thanks God for that, putt he must not rise in agitation against the hands or stewards of Providence that do him goot whatefer.

"A little steepend will do ferry well for a single man, and that's the reason that priests and pachelor ministers can afford to join the Land Leaguers, for they are all right if they ket a little cream for their tea from a neighbour, which is quite easy whatefer. Putt, as I was saying, what can these pachelors understand apout keeping a wife, and ketting food, and clothes, and shoes, and pooks, and education, for a houseful of children? It is not at all easy for a married minister who has a large family, and only a small steepend, to pe a Land Leaguer, for you see the competition for situations is now so ferry fearful, that, unless one has a letter of recommendation from a landlord, or one of the gentry, it is impossible to get into any post of any kind whatefer, or into a shop or office in Glasgow or Edinburgh or London, or any goot post aproad.

"In the olden time, when wars were always plentiful, and fighting men much required by the landlords, the assistance of the clergy for enlisting was necessary whatefer; and it was then that they could ferry easily get posts for their sons, in return for such assistance. And when the recruiting officers came round, there was always a Shance of Ketting one of the taughters *enlisted* too! for the kirls are ferry fond of *joining* the army whatefer! And the minister whose taughter got puckled with a red-coat officer was sure to procure plenty of recruits, so as to earn promotion for his son-in-law! and he would then pray more fervently for our *King and country* whatefer, and against *our enemies.*

"Plenty of enemies were always made in those tays, to keep the wars koing, in order to maintain the price of krain at a shenteel figure, so that there would pe no risk of the rents of land falling whatefer! For you see the ministers' steepends would fall too, if the price of krain came down, and thus the gentry and clergy peing in the same poat, you see, would sink together. And the poor, who are always poor, would not pe a pit the petter whatefer, put on the contrary, much worser, pecause the gentry and the clergy would pe less able to kive them the usual *charity!* And it is here one can see ferry clearly, the wickedness of the repeal of the *Corn Laws,* which kave a kreat plow to *charity,* and other forms of holiness!

"This *innovation* apout the *Corn Laws* led to Poor Rates and Poor Houses, which is no charity whatefer. We are now koing on to Free Education all round, with, no toubt, the Universities thrown open to the Public; and all the Professors made to teach, not only the sons, but also the taughters of the people at large, which will testroy ferry much the educational status of the *gentry* whatefer.

"Indeed if the Radicals get much more of their own way they will pass an Act of Parliament for having efery pody porn into the world with equal rights to eferything, and even the most sacred rights which the landlords hafe to the land will be *controverted!* and all rents, and, may pe, all tithes too, *confiscated* - among the community at large.

"There is no toubt these things are coming fast, for the young clergy are peginning to pe ferry radical whatefer, and they now lay kreat stress on the words: *That God is no respecter of persons,* and such like Piple texts, without modifying them in any way py the *Confession of Faith.* And, in like manner, they fix upon the words *Thy Kingdom come: Thy Will be done ON THE EARTH, as it is in heaven.* For, you see, there will pe no landlords there whatefer! Now

169

this is a kreat *innovation!* So, who can tell what may come to pass within a few years? Perhaps, even the Free Church minister of Strathconon may pe seen joining in a *teer raid* before long!

"It is the wicked *Land Leaguers* that are to plame for kiving such tangerous knowledge to the people, for the 'agitation' has stirred them up to make inquiry apout *all* their rights; and the *Free Church* which stood up for the apolition of Church-lordisrn in 1843, is put into a strange fix as to the apolition of land-lordism now. The *Free Church* is in kreat tanger whatefer - all caused py that radical Patronage Act of 1874.

"The changes that are now taking place are ferry extraordinary, when we consider how the landed gentry and the clergy worked hand in hand in times of old. Things were not so hard on the clergy even in more recent times, as they are now. And I'll tell you apout that. My wife is a Minister's taughter, and my wife's mother happened to pe a natural taughter of the Laird himself. How strange Providence is! especially when there's a woman mixed up with it, which is ferry often the case.

"Well, my wife's father's family was ferry little trouple to him whatefer, for they kot education and situations ferry easily in those tays. And one of them, named Angus, who did not care apout college education, went to Australia, and kot on ferry well, and has thirty thousand sheep - he and another who was only a Crofter's son here. And they hafe more land between them there than the Tuke of Sutherland has here. He was home the other year, and he is a terrible Land Leaguer. He said that the Crofters and the people were kreat fools to leave the land with the Tuke of Sutherland or any other landlord whatefer. This is what Angus used to say! Pefore the *Crofters' Act* was passed he said that, and nopody pelieved him then whatefer, except the agitators, who took for Kospel efery word he said. Angus was a kreat Radical, although he was a minister's son.

"There was another curious thing: there was the woman who was the mother of my wife's mother, you know. Well, you understand, the laird was a ferry kind-hearted man, and tid not put her away empty whatefer. And with the money he kave her she married a shepherd, who was a sort of an Englishman, prought here to set agoing the sheep-farming, for they were just evicting the Highlanders on account of the sheep craze at the time. Well, she and this shepherd kot a whole desolated klen as a *tack* to themselves. And some of their tescendants are the piggest *tacksmen* today in the whole Highlands, and hafe plenty of money yet, although they lost a lot of it on sheep not long ago. And the tescendants of the laird who kave the first money to their kreat-krandmother are now quite empty. Putt still money is not everything.

"And here we see how ferry strange the Providence of God works. For, there was so much cruelty and oppression tone at that time to

171

thousands, who were evicted; and God - who is always a ferry just God, howefer difficult He is sometimes to understand - saw it just, and - as it were - more expedient, and even more merciful, to distripute the punishment among the tescendants of the men who tid, or helped to do, that mischief. Providence is a ferry strange thing in visiting the iniquity of the fathers upon the sons and more generations pesides, and that is often ferry clearly to pe seen with regard to evictions. For how could God make full justice to the thousands who were oppressed, and whose tescendants also suffered, if he wasn't to extend the punishment to the tescendants of the oppressors whatefer? And this is the way God paffles all the philosophers, who try to understand things which they cannot understand!

"Now, although I hafe, as a minister, to keep town all *agitation*, I must show a sort of sympathy with it: and notwithstanding it is the Kospel of peace I always preach, still I must sympathise *in reality* with those who come to look at the land, and at the ruins of the old twellings, from which their ancestors, or maybe their parents, or themselves when children were evicted. It would be a kreat wonder if these were not Land Leaguers whatefer. Even my own poys are krowing up on the side of the *agitation* in spite of me - especially since that visit of their uncle from Australia. And what do you think of more than one of my taughters turning Land Leaguers too? They nefer kot over the 'prisoning of the Skye and Clashmore women, and the poinding py Lord MacTonal of that papy *at a sixpence whatefer!* For they tell me to my face that that papy had a soul as valuable as a papy born to Lord MacTonal himself, and perhaps a body as goot, if not petter, too. After *that,* the whole country pecame Land Leaguers, and I myself had to attend their meetings, otherwise my congregation would not come near my church whatefer.

"And the agitation grew so strong in the Lewis, with police, soldiers, marines, and *teer raiders,* that Lady Matheson at last ran away and left the island there! But she was no ferry wise whatefer; for when the crofters and cottars came to her with some grievance, she stamped her foot, and said this, in the face of the people: "The land is mine, and I can do with it as I like!" And the police, and soldiers, and marines were of ferry little use whatefer, except for helping on the agitation.

"By the way, it was at King's College, Aberdeen, that my wife's father studied, and he had many stories apout all the Professors there, although I forget their names. If my wife's prother, William, who tied only a year ago, was alive, I am sure he could tell something apout such a man as Professor Ogilvie, for he knew all his father's old stories. I remember hearing apout a ferry radical Aberdeen Professor of that time, who had to do with the innovation which spoilt the Universities. Now, that unjust and wicked innovation was fully as pad as the *Crofters Act* of 1886.

"Look on England - there is no land agitation there whatefer! For they have still *conserved* all the privileges of Oxford and Cambridge for the nobility and gentry, and that's the reason why so many of the English, who ton't pelong to the *privileged* classes, have to send their poys to the Scottish Universities; while at the same time the sons of the Scottish nobility and gentry are enjoying all the endowments and privileges of Oxford and Cambridge. Putt things in England may go ferry wrong soon too, for they took in Professor Robertson Smith there, after he was put out of the Free Church College of Aberdeen. For you see, that innovation about colleges and education is the first step of the mischief, and it will pe a wonder if Professor Robertson Smith refrains from writing a Land League pook too. That indeed would be a kreat tanger not only to England and Ireland but to Scotland as well, pecause the Scots, except ferry few, tid not pelieve in his new toctrines apout Moses, putt if he turned a Land Leaguer, like Moses himself, all the highlanders would then pelieve in him whatefer. You see clearly how that old radical Professor Ogilvie who pegan the innovations of the Aberdeen Colleges was also the author of a Land League pook.

"Putt he tid a much wickeder thing than that, when he wrote a jubilee treatise on the Land Laws of Moses. And it is a ferry tangerous argument to say that *Jesus came to fulfil those Laws*, and that efery landlord must "return efery man into his possession" *of the land*, all in accordance with chapter xxv. of *Leviticus*. The parable of the Tuke of Argyll - who is a *Campbell!* - having *to go through the eye of a needle,* is also a ferry wicked argument whatefer. And, moreofer, it is ferry much against the *Confession of Faith* to say that the clergy, after the example of Jesus, should try to save the souls of the rich py advising them to kive up all their lands to the industrious poor, whose labour *earned* the wrongly-called *'un*-earned increment' of the value of such lands. For this is the Kospel *Notice to quit!* And to the clergy who fail to deliver this *Notice,* and to the landlords who fail to obey it, the Lord says: - "If ye will not be reformed by me by these things, but will walk contrary unto me; then will I also walk contrary unto you, and will punish you yet seven times for your sins. And I will make your cities waste, and bring your sanctuaries into desolation" - all as foretold in chapter xxvi. of *Leviticus,* which raises a ferry difficult point in the minds of all those who pelieve in the Scottish *Confession of Faith,* and in the English and Irish *Faiths* too, more especially on account of the French Revolution fulfilment of that ferry old law *.

" I have seen some nations like o'erloaded asses
Kick off their burthens - meaning the high classes. "

---

* Lord Macaulay, speaking in the British House of Commons, on Parliamentary Reform in 1831, appealed to the English Aristocracy, to take warning by the fate of the *noblesse* of France. "And why", asked Macaulay, "were those haughty nobles destroyed with that utter destruction? Why were they scattered over the face of the earth, their titles abolished, their escutcheons defaced, their parks wasted, their palaces dismantled. their heritage given to strangers? Because they had no sympathy with the people, no discernment of the signs of the times; because, in the pride and narrowness of their hearts, they called those whose warning might have saved them, theorists and speculators; because they refused all concession till the time had arrived when no concession would avail."

"Putt, as I was going to say, the story of Professor Ogilvie's *Essay* on the Land Question, written in Scotland apout the year 1781, is ferry strange, and prings to my mind a difficulty my wife and myself always had apout Purns and his *Twa Dogs*. Where tid Purns get all his information apout the *outs* and *ins* of the private life of the shentry, and how they lived aproad too? My wife always pelieved that *Caesar* was a real man, and, moreofer, a real shentleman too, who knew from his own observation all apout the ways of the shentry. She thinks he was a confidential friend of Purns -

" Nae doubt but they were fain o' ither,
An' unco pack and thick thegither " -

and that Purns disguised him as well as he could py saying that:

- " he was nane o' Scotland's dogs,
But whalpet some place far abroad,
Where sailors gang to fish for cod. "

"After that arch Land Leaguer, Henry George, came ofer to this country, I used to say to my wife: 'There's your *Caesar* now!'. And I myself looked upon his coming from America to *Caesarize* us *à la Purns*, as a sort of prophecy fulfilled, putt the answer I always kot from my wife was 'Fiddlesticks!' Now if I tell her that Professor Ogilvie was a Land Leaguer and a contemporary of Purns, she will at once say that he was *Caesar* whatefer. You know how strange women are for shumping at conclusions!

"Well, shust to try her, I'll not tell her a word, at first, apout what sort of a man Professor Ogilvie was. I'll not say that he was of the real *landed shentry* or that he was the 'shentleman and scholar' who acted as travelling tutor to the Tuke of Gordon on a grand tour of Europe, which tour is so vividly pictured in the *Twa Dogs* as to suggest the pencil of an eye-witness - a philosophical Land-law-reforming eye!

"Of course I'll tell her all these things quietly and py degrees. Putt there is one thing I'll tell her ferry cautiously whatefer, namely this - that it was in the same year (1786) Purns wrote and published his *Twa Dogs*, and Professor Ogilvie wrote and published his *plan of campaign* against the *Highland shentry and klergy*, for the apolition and confiscation of their own College at Aberdeen, which, pefore his innovations, was generally known as *The Highland University*.

"Were I to tell her that Professor Ogilvie had a kreat affection for pastoral poets like Virgil, and that he was ferry fond of Horace and Ovid, and that he was 'tinctured with the sublime melancholy of Ossian', she would at once conclude that he, when maturing his *plan*, in that year, 1786, must have visited his academic friends in Glasgow, for it was the Glasgow University he took as his model for the proposed *united* University of Aberdeen. She could ferry easily put me in a corner by asking me, whether I thought any reasonable person could imagine that a Land Leaguer and a lover of pastoral poetry like

177

Professor Ogilvie could refrain from going the length of Ayrshire to visit another Land Leaguer, and a maker, as well as a lover, of pastoral poetry? You see *I* could not say '*Fiddlesticks*' to that whatefer. Professor Ogilvie had his knife ready for the 'Highland Gentry' at that time, as shown by his *Plan of Campaign*, which came out in print on the 20th of July, 1786. And it was 'upon a bonie day *in June*', 1786, that the *Twa Dogs*:

> " began a lang digression
> About the LORDS O' THE CREATION. "

"I'll pe ferry careful in discussing dates with her whatefer.   For Purns also had his knife in the *Highland gentry* at that time; which comes out ferry clearly in the *Address of Beelzebub* on the 1st of June, 1786, putt kept from being published until 1818; and the true story of it is still expunged from all editions *for the people!* You see the Glengarry men revolted against their Chief in 1786 pecause he took all their lands from them.   Eviction was the reward they received for fighting under the false colours of British Liberty in the American War of Independence.   They fought for the liberty of landlordism - *the liberty to evict* - and they got it!

"Other chiefs, on hearing that the Glengarry men resolved to emigrate to America, "agreed to co-operate with Government" to prevent by force these landless Highlanders from emigrating "*in search of their natural rights!*" It was this that moved Purns to write: -

' *To the Right Honourable the Earl of Breadalbane, President of the Right Honourable and Honourable the Highland Society, which met on the 23rd of May last (1786) at the Shakespeare, Covent Garden,* to concert ways and means to frustrate the design of five hundred Highlanders, who, *as the Society were informed by Mr Mackenzie of Applecross,* were so audacious as to attempt an escape from their lawful lords and masters, whose property they were, *by emigrating from the lands of Mr McDonald of Glengarry to the wilds of Canada,* in search of that fantastic thing * - LIBERTY. ' †

"In the following year, 1787, when addressing the water-fowl of Loch Turrit, the poet's eye was evidently still fixed on the Glengarry *exodus:* -

" Swiftly seek, on clanging wings,
Other lakes and other springs,
And the foe you cannot brave,
Scorn at least to be his slave. "

"Were it not that my wife was always ferry fond of Purns, I would pe as ignorant of him as any other Free Church Minister in the Highlands whatefer. For it is always our recognised duty to put in the fire efery copy of Purns, or such pooks, we get hold of in the hands of our people. Putt this copy of Purns my wife has is a ferry old one that has pelonged to her mother, which was always kept locked up;

---

* Compare these words with Professor Ogilvie's phrase - 'in search of their natural rights'.

† See "Address to Beelzebub", as cited.

and my wife got a hold of it when her mother tied. She also keeps it locked up. And we must not read it, except on the sly, so that nopody discovers there is a Purns in the Free Manse whatefer. The people are so treadfully prejudiced, ever since the old *moderate* ministers taught them that prejudice.

"And there is no *agitation* in our district except on the part of some radical Protestant crofters and two or three Catholics, who assert and maintain that the land was originally appropriated by spoliation and robbery, and that the landlords have no right to it whatefer; and they say it is the Teffil, and not Providence, that worked all the mischief; and they call the priest and myself the Teffil's agents too, and they look upon the *Crofters' Act* as real Providence from God in their favour. And they say that the doctrine preached in favour of landlordism is ferry much opposed to the Law of Moses, and, moreover, that it is quite contrary to the letter, as well as the spirit, of the Gospel of Jesus. They also say that all those who pray, "Thy kingdom come: Thy will be done on earth as it is in heaven", but who nevertheless stand by, and do nothing to disapprove of rack rents, evictions, and other oppressions *on the earth*, are not much petter than Judas Iscariot; and moreover, that Christianity has been abused as a pretext for war, slavery, and landlordism for a ferry long time."

" *The State assumes the right of eminent domain over its territorial basis, whereby every landholder becomes in theory a tenant of the State. In its capacity as ultimate landlord, the State confers two distinct monopolies, entirely different in their nature. The one is a monopoly of the use-value of land; and the other, a monopoly of the economic rent of land. The first gives the right to keep other persons from using the land in question and the right to exclusive possession of values accruing from the application of labour to it; values, that is, which are produced by exercise of the economic means upon the particular property in question. Monopoly of economic rent, on the other hand, gives the exclusive right to values accruing from the desire of other persons to possess that property; values which take their rise irrespective of any exercise of the economic means on the part of the holder. Economic rent arises when, for whatever reason, two or more persons compete for the possession of a piece of land, and it increases directly according to the number of persons competing.*

" *The first postulate of fundamental economics is that man is a land-animal, deriving his subsistence wholly from the land (as a technical term in economics, land includes all natural resources, earth, air, water, sunshine, timber and minerals in situ, etc.). His entire wealth is produced by the application of labour and capital to land; no form of wealth known to man can be produced in any other way. Hence, if his free access to land be shut off by legal preemption, he can apply his labour and capital only with the landholder's consent, and on the landholder's terms; in other words, it is at this point, and at this point only, that exploitation becomes practicable. Hence there is actually no such thing as a "labour-problem", for no encroachment on the rights of either labour or capital can possibly take place until all natural resources within reach have been preempted. What we call the "problem of the unemployed" is in no sense a problem, but a direct consequence of State-created monopoly. Therefore the first concern of the State must be invariably, as we find it invariably is, with its policy of land-tenure.*"

AJ Nock *Our Enemy the State*

The Global Green *Tax?*

Community Ground Rent

by
Peter Gibb

Community Ground Rent is such a simple measure, and such a *just* one. Could it not be supported by folk of *all* political persuasions? '*Honest* Capitalism'? '*True* Socialism'? A '*green*' land and tax policy you say?! But Community Ground Rent is not actually a tax at all !! - it is a *user fee*.

Who would call the coin put in a parking meter a tax? - Nor is it one: it is a *fee*, for the exclusive use of a certain area of the Queen's highway, for a certain period of time - and just so Community Ground Rent for land. It is a simple payment for real value directly received.

We are used to considering the normal source of public revenue as taxes, which necessarily harm us. Taxes on labour stifle enterprise: taxes on capital stifle investment; taxes on goods stifle trade - and the existing tax structure not only distorts production and distribution, it also depresses land values and rents. As a proportion of the national incomes of Western societies, under present tax regimes, the underlying total value of land rents is between a quarter and a third 1 : therefore land rents would be well able to support necessary state expenditure, in a prosperous society with full employment. Just as all right-founded enterprises fund their activities from the resources they rightly have at hand, so it is right to source our public expenditure from our public resources - the common fund of every community in the land, given us by Nature and made valuable by the community. And relative to current tax systems, Community Ground Rent would be simple to administer, with liability hard to avoid.

Community Ground Rent would be assessed annually, holding by holding, by a Public Valuer, and would be payable by the land holder to the community. Assessments would be based on the 'unimproved' value of the site - that is, the bare site value *exclusive of all 'improvements'* (such as buildings, cultivation, etc.), which are the result of man's labour, and therefore private.

---

1   *Costing the Earth*, edited by R Banks. (See Further Reading).

Community Ground Rent would be inherently place-based, and so eminently suitable as a *decentralised* revenue system (where authorities could collect funds locally, and pass grants *up to* central government). Community Ground Rent is truly the practical, effective, and inexpensive - as well as being the *naturally just* - means of meeting common public expenses.

The introduction of such a fundamental measure as Community Ground Rent would obviously have many and far-reaching consequences for a country like Scotland. They would include: the *systematic* restoration of a more just distribution of wealth, and the fading away of social inequity (of both opportunity and reward, which today breeds such contrasting extremes of wealth and poverty) - rather than its progressive entrenchment as at present; current taxes could be reduced or even abolished; today's depression and distortion of the economics of production and distribution, where taxes stifle the incentive to work, save and trade, would lessen or disappear; the system of public finance would become more transparent, accountable and acceptable; labour wages and returns on savings would increase; land could no longer be the subject of profitable speculative investment by commercial interests - and would appeal less for unsocial amusement -   prompting a fall in land prices and, while the market settled, an increase in the amount of land offered for sale; the national economy would stabilise, with the breaking of the interminable cycle of economic boom and bust (which is *actually* based on land speculation); landholders would be encouraged to optimise returns from their holding (within, just as today, a system of planning and environmental regulation) - so encouraging community development, and decreasing involuntary unemployment; land parcels would be disaggregated, in the shedding of underused 'investment liabilities', so holding size would naturally decrease and total numbers increase, both effects easing the passage to land-ownership for the many, not the few; the initiative for enterprise and development, and the power to let or make it happen, would tend to remain with, or revert to, local individuals and groups.

So is it a wonder that man is not working now to transform his societies in the light of the truths shown us by Ogilvie? The fact is that, deep down, he is. All over the world, small groups of people are coming together and realising that the value of the rent of the land *is* the natural, lawful, proper and practical source for meeting our common public expenses. They have seen that the private appropriation of the value of the land *is indeed* "a gross and blasphemous slander on the Creator, as well as a most iniquitous fraud on the bulk of mankind"[2]. Henry George said it a hundred years ago: William Ogilvie said it two hundred years ago: Moses said it three thousand years ago: - but, **today**, they are saying it in Russia [3], in South Africa [4], in Denmark [5], in the USA [6], in the UN [7] . . .

. . . and in *Scotland* ???

" *You cannot cure this deep-seated disease by any half-way measures. You must go to the root, boldly and firmly. Take no stock of those people who preach moderation. Moderation is not what is needed; it is religious indignation. Grasp your thistle. Proclaim the grand truth that every human being born in Scotland has an inalienable and equal right to the soil of Scotland - a right that no law can do away with.* "

Henry George *Scotland and Scotsmen*

2   See the concluding lines of MacDonald's *Biographical Notes* (p. 159).

3   "A glimpse of what is in store for Russia surfaced in a key report to the Habitat conference in Istanbul this week. The United Nations document concludes that structural adjustment programs imposed by the International Monetary Fund are a main reason for the deterioration in the social fabric of the world's cities. These programs, which include the privatisation of land and natural resources, have increased poverty, homelessness and unemployment in more than 50 countries that borrowed from the IMF, reports the UN.

"At a Duma congress in Moscow on May 21, (we) issued a similar warning to the deputies who were about to give the third reading to the Land Code.... Why do we fear the Land Code? Because it threatens the return of landlordism.... Russia deserves better." *A Tolstoyan Land Code* by Fred Harrison. 'The Moscow Times', June 7, 1996.

4   "Serious thought is being given to ... a Rural Land Tax in the RSA. This is being investigated by the department of Land Affairs and a Parliamentary Select Committee on Land Affairs. The subject is also just starting to enter into public dialogue and the press.... Over the last few months there have been numerous reports in the media regarding the intention of the Minister to introduce a rural land tax, but the details have not been set out. Godfrey Dunkley had a long meeting with minister Derek Hanekom on March 7th 1995 during which strong emphasis was placed on the need for such a tax to apply to all land and not only farming land. It was also pointed out that this should not be seen as an additional tax but that an equivalent amount should be off-set against taxes that impinge at the margin of production." From *A Rural Land Tax For The Republic Of South Africa*, in the 'Association for Incentive Taxation Revenue Research Newsletter' No. 8, June 1995.

5   "... A Georgist political party was created, referred to in English as the Justice Party, which in 1926, won two seats in the Danish Parliament.

" 'The greatest success of the Justice Party occurred in 1957. The party won nine seats in the Parliament; and, through an alliance with two other minority parties, was actually in a controlling position. Viggo Starcke declared that he had the 'honor' to be the parliamentary leader of the Justice Party for fourteen years.

" 'The three years of 1957-1960 were years of success for the Justice Party'. Viggo Starcke remembered: 'The results for the country were good.... There was progress in every sphere of economic life. Production rose ... more than 30%. Savings, especially in the private sector, increased enormously ... taxes were reduced, so that a family which in 1960 had the same income ... as in 1957, had a tax reduction of more than 10%.... In 1957 Denmark had considerable unemployment. In 1960 the unemployment had given way to full employment.... Twice the law concerning taxes on unearned increment was improved.... The results were good for the country. ... For the Justice Party they were not. At the election of 1960 the party was defeated and lost all of its members in the Parliament. The result was unfair. It was mainly due to two sets of factors. The first was the continued, organised attacks from the parties representing big money and great monopolies.' " From *The Decline and Fall of Georgism: A New Modest Proposal* by Jack Schwartzman, (paper delivered at Den Danske Henry George Forening International Conference, Roskilde, Denmark, 1995), citing *Centuries of Experience with Land Taxation in Denmark,* by Viggo Starcke, Henry George Forlaget, 1967 & 1995.

6 "There is continuity in history. A spontaneous, unbroken thread runs through it.

"The simple nature of that thread is the gradual unfolding of an idea: that human beings must be accorded respect as individuals and that each and every one of us is equally free.... Personal commitment (to this idea) got me elected in 1992 as a legislator: as a Representative to New Hampshire's General Court.... New Hampshire can accurately be called "the most nearly (Henry) Georgist" state among the 50 which are united in North America. We have unusually few taxes that fall on labour and industry. There is neither a general sales nor a general income tax among them. We depend more heavily than any other state - by a substantial margin - upon the property tax. We are making headway toward assessing land at its market value, thereby taking the measure of economic rent. And we tax our citizens less heavily, as a percentage of per capita income, than do any of the other states.

"I spend most of my waking hours these days looking for ways to convince my colleagues to take those few remaining steps that will make us truly Georgist, and authentically a "single tax" state." From *Property Rights: A Common-Sensism,* by Richard Noyes, (Paper delivered at Den Danske Henry George Forening International Conference, Roskilde, Denmark, 1995).

7 The following are excerpts from three recent UN Resolutions:

"We urge relevant UN agencies to study alternative methods of taxation, including land value taxation which would shift taxation policies off labour and productive capital and onto the common heritage of land and natural resources, so as to promote a more equitable distribution of wealth around the Earth."

"Base development policy on an ethic of fair and equal rights to the Earth for all human beings; promote collecting for the community as a whole the increase in ground rent that results from sustainable development."

"Develop education of alternative economic systems, eg., replace taxation with payments to local governments for services rendered to the site."

Further Reading

The following publications are available post-free from Land Reform Scotland *(see list of addresses overleaf).*

Progress and Poverty (super-cond.)	Henry George	50p
Scotland and Scotsmen	"	£1.50
Principles for Land Reform		£1.50
The Law of Rent and Wages		50p

The following publications are available from the Henry George Foundation *(see list of addresses overleaf).*

BOOKS

Progress and Poverty	Henry George
Social Problems	"
Protection or Free Trade	"
The Science of Political Economy	"
Commons Without Tragedy	Ed. RV Andelson
Costing the Earth	Ed. Ronald Banks
The Power in the Land	Fred Harrison
The Recovery Myth -A Positive Response	Bryan Kavanagh
Freedom - the Only End	F McEachran
Now the Synthesis. Capitalism, Socialism and the New Social Contract	Ed. Richard Noyes
The Broken Trust	Edgar Buck
Land, People and Politics	Roy Douglas
A Philosophy for a Fair Society	Michael Hudson, GJ Miller & Kris Feder
The Corruption of Economics	Mason Gaffney & Fred Harrison
Land and Taxation	Ed. N Tideman
Our Enemy the State (currently unavailable)	AJ Nock
Land of Freedom	Fred Harrison
Why the German Republic Fell	Bruno Heilig

PERIODICALS

Land and Liberty
Practical Politics (Ph. 01494 522856)
The Land is Ours (Ph. 01865 722016)

Addresses

Land Reform Scotland
The Chalmer, Mill of Towie, Cullen,
Buckie, Banffshire, Scotland.

Henry George Foundation
177, Vauxhall Bridge Road,
London, SW1V 1EU, England.

Land Policy Council
7, Kings Road, Teddington,
TW11 0QB, England.

The Land is Ours
Box E, 111 Magdalen Road, Oxford
OX4 1RQ, England.
http://www.oneworld.org/tlio

Robert Schalkenbach Foundation
41, East 72nd Street, New York,
NY 10021, USA.